ROBINSON

Contents

Multiple choice

Choose the correct answer.

1. A number exactly divisible by 3
   - (a) 52
   - (b) 50
   - (c) 42

2. Subtract 19 from 100.
   - (a) 91
   - (b) 81
   - (c) 71

3. A square number
   - (a) 49
   - (b) 48
   - (c) 50

4. $\frac{3}{4}$ of a metre
   - (a) 75 cm
   - (b) 25 cm
   - (c) 80 cm

5. Centimetres in $2\frac{1}{2}$ metres
   - (a) 250 cm
   - (b) 200 cm
   - (c) 205 cm

6. In the number 3627, the six is worth
   - (a) 60
   - (b) 600
   - (c) 6000

7. Half of 1
   - (a) $\frac{1}{2}$
   - (b) $\frac{1}{4}$
   - (c) $\frac{3}{4}$

8. $\frac{1}{2}$ kg is the same as
   - (a) 1000 g
   - (b) 500 g
   - (c) 200 g

9. Which is largest?
   - (a) 7×8
   - (b) 9×6
   - (c) 5×10

10. 1 more than 989
   - (a) 990
   - (b) 1000
   - (c) 999

11. $\frac{1}{4}$ l is the same as
   - (a) 500 ml
   - (b) 750 ml
   - (c) 250 ml

12. $\frac{1}{4}$ of £1
   - (a) 75p
   - (b) 50p
   - (c) 25p

13. 45 minutes after 2.45

   (a) 3.20

   (b) 3.30

   (c) 3.40

14. $\frac{1}{2}$ is the same as

   (a) $\frac{4}{8}$

   (b) $\frac{6}{8}$

   (c) $\frac{4}{10}$

15. $2\frac{1}{2}$ is the same as

   (a) 2·2

   (b) 2·8

   (c) 2·5

16. Which is smallest?

   (a) $2\frac{3}{10}$

   (b) $1\frac{3}{4}$

   (c) 2·1

17. Double 65.

   (a) 120

   (b) 130

   (c) 135

18. 280 divided by 10

   (a) 14

   (b) 25

   (c) 28

19. A rectangle is a

   (a) quadrilateral

   (b) triangle

   (c) pentagon

20. 13 multiplied by 10

   (a) 103

   (b) 130

   (c) 113

21. $\frac{1}{2}$ hr after 2.50 pm

   (a) 3.10 pm

   (b) 2.20 pm

   (c) 3.20 pm

22. 99 less than 740

   (a) 639

   (b) 641

   (c) 699

23. $\frac{3}{5}$ is the same as

   (a) $\frac{6}{10}$

   (b) $\frac{8}{10}$

   (c) $\frac{1}{2}$

24. Double £3·99

   (a) £7·92

   (b) £6·99

   (c) £7·98

Number and Algebra

Write the answers only.

1. 264 + 99	2. 306 + 99	3. 514 + 99	4. 185 + 99
5. 462 − 99	6. 308 − 99	7. 947 − 99	8. 838 − 99
9. 164 × 10	10. 138 × 10	11. 200 × 10	12. 946 × 10
13. 230 ÷ 10	14. 140 ÷ 10	15. 389 ÷ 10	16. 473 ÷ 10

Set these out in the way you find easiest.

17. 643 + 27 + 196   18. 749 + 1006 + 9

19. 402 + 1398 + 16   20. 609 − 416

21. 906 − 387   22. 4000 − 3629

23. 602 × 5   24. 1097 × 4

25. 278 × 9   26. 1175 × 8

27. 392 ÷ 7   28. 718 ÷ 3

29. 256 ÷ 8   30. 253 ÷ 6

31. John has £1·36.
Jane has 3 times as much.
How much has Jane?

32. Jenny has £4·70 in her
money box.
It is in 10p pieces.
How many coins in her money box?

33. Anne's shoes cost £14·50.
Lynne's shoes cost £11·75.
How much dearer were
Anne's shoes?

Mr. Green is a gardener.

1. He grew his tomato plants in boxes.
   Each box had 12 plants.
   How many plants in 9 boxes?

2. He grew 108 pansies.
   He planted half of them.
   He sold the rest.
   How many did he sell?

3. He sells damsons.
   He charges 50p for a kilogram.
   How much will 14 kg cost?

4. He bought 10 packets of seeds.
   Each packet cost 39p.
   How much did he spend on seeds?

5. He bought a new spade and fork.
   The spade cost £14·50.
   The fork cost £12·50.
   How much did he spend?

6. His watering can cost £3·75.
   He paid with a £10 note.
   How much change did he get?

7. The watering can holds 9 litres
   of water.
   He filled it 4 times.
   How much water did he use?

Digit cards 0–9

Each of the digit cards has a home.
Find it.

1.
$$
\begin{array}{r}
2\;\square \\
+\;2\;\square \\
\hline
\square\;4
\end{array}
$$

2.
$$
\begin{array}{r}
\square\;\square \\
-\;\square\;3 \\
\hline
1\;1
\end{array}
$$

3.
$$
\begin{array}{r}
3\;8 \\
-\;1\;\square \\
\hline
2\;\square
\end{array}
$$

4.
$$
\begin{array}{r}
4\;\square \\
+\;2\;\square \\
\hline
6\;9
\end{array}
$$

Calculator

Make the number on each display. You can only use the keys shown.

1.

2.

3.

4.

5.

6.

7.

8.

9.

Set of rails	£12·50 a set
Engines	£15·50 each
Carriages	£2·25 each
Trucks	£1·95 each
Signals	£1·80 each
Station platforms	£2·80 a pair
Bridges	£2·35 each

1. Tina bought a new engine and carriage for her train set.
   How much did it cost her?

2. Peter bought 2 new carriages and 2 new trucks.
   How much did he spend?

3. David had 3 new signals and a pair of platforms.
   How much did he pay?

4. Paula had a new engine and a new bridge.
   What was the total cost?

5. Alison bought 4 carriages.
   How much change did she get from a £10 note?

6. Keith added a new set of rails to his train set.
   He only had £10·75.
   How much did his father lend him?

7. John had no bridges in his train set.
   He had £10 to spend. How many bridges could he buy?
   How much would he have left over?

At this restaurant meals are served at mid-day and in the evening. This table shows how many people had a meal at the restaurant during one week.

	Sun	Mon	Tues	Wed	Thurs	Fri	Sat
Mid-day	84	48	55	73	65	49	32
Evening	79	63	49	84	72	89	94

1. How many mid-day meals were served that week?

2. How many evening meals were served?

3. Which was the busiest day?

4. On which day were fewest meals served?

5. How many meals were served altogether?

6. Mid-day meals were £3 each.
   Evening meals were £6 each.
   How much money was collected during the week?

9

Peg board, pegs, squared paper

1. Copy these triangle patterns on a peg board.
   Make the next two patterns in this series.
   Write the number of pegs in each pattern.

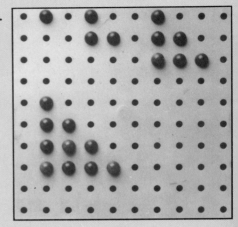

2. Write the next four numbers in this series:
   1, 3, 6, ...
   These numbers are called
   triangular numbers.

Cut these shapes out of squared paper.
Cut out the next two shapes in this series.

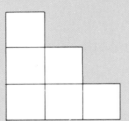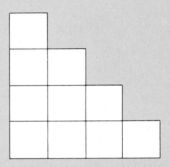

3. Count the number of squares in each shape.
   What are these numbers called?

   Arrange the shapes in pairs to make squares.
   Stick the completed squares in your book.

4. What kind of number do you get if you add any
   two adjacent triangular numbers?

5. Write the first six square numbers.
   Find the difference between adjacent ones.
   What are these numbers called?

Cut out 6 identical hexagons.
Number them like this:

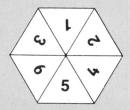
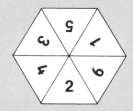
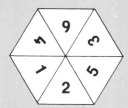

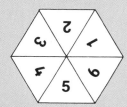
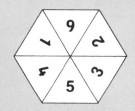
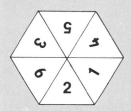

Tessellate the hexagons to make this shape.
Where hexagons touch, the numbers must match.

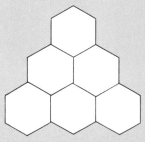

Rearrange the numbers in these hexagons so
adjacent hexagons have a difference of
at least 3.

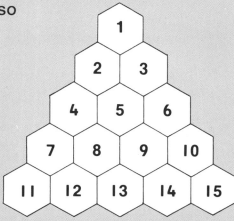

Measures

What are the readings shown?

1.

2.

3.

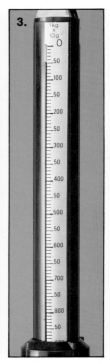

4.

5.

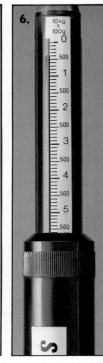

6.

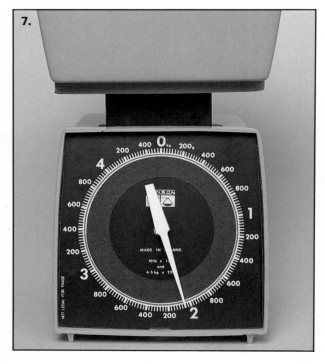

7.

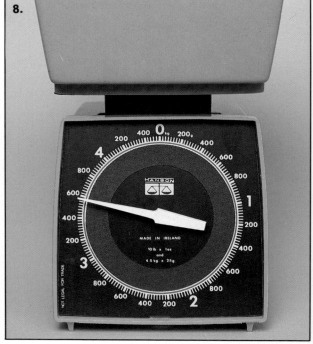

8.

Spring-balance, scales, bathroom scales

Find 6 things to weigh using a spring-balance.
Estimate the weight of each object.
Weigh each object.
Record your results in a table.

Object	Estimate	Weight

Now find 6 things to weigh using scales.
Estimate the weight of each object.
Weigh each object.
Record your results in a table.

Object	Estimate	Weight

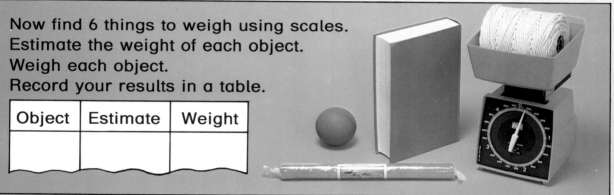

Estimate the weight of 6 friends.
Weigh them.
Record your results in a table.

Name	Estimate	Weight

13

> Remember: 1000 g = 1 kg
> 1450 g = 1·450 kg

1. Complete this table.

g	kg
1375	1·375
2030	
	0·750
3445	
	2·125
740	

Put these weights in order
from smallest to largest.
It may help to write each weight in g.

2. 450 g, $\frac{1}{2}$ kg, 0·405 kg

3. $1\frac{1}{4}$ kg, 1·205 kg, 1025 g

4. 2·705 kg, 2570 g, $2\frac{3}{4}$ kg

5. $\frac{3}{4}$ kg, 800 g, 0·705 kg

Which of these weights is the most sensible?

6.

46 kg
4·600 kg
460 kg

7.

0·200 kg
2 kg
20 kg

8.

275 g
2·750 kg
27 kg

9. 540 g + 390 g + 850 g

10. 880 g + 450 g + 540 g

11. 530 g × 4

12. 650 g × 8

13. Double $\frac{3}{4}$ kg.

14. Halve $1\frac{3}{4}$ kg.

Measures

Remember: 1000 ml = 1 l
1240 ml = 1·240 l

1. Complete this table.

ml	l
950	0·950
1400	
	2·375
2050	
	3·515
4350	

Put these capacities in order, starting with the largest.
It may help to write each capacity in ml.

2. 705 ml, $\frac{3}{4}$ l, 0·780 l

3. $1\frac{1}{4}$ l, 1215 ml, 1·125 l

4. 2·225 l, $2\frac{1}{2}$ l, 2550 ml

5. $1\frac{3}{4}$ l, 1·800 l, 1650 ml

Which of these capacities is the most sensible?

6.

5 l
500 l
50 l

7.

50 ml
5 ml
500 ml

8.

20 ml
2 l
$\frac{1}{2}$ l

9. 540 ml + 390 ml + 850 ml

10. 850 ml + 740 ml + 560 ml

11. 350 ml × 9

12. 460 ml × 5

13. Halve $1\frac{1}{4}$ l.

14. Double $1\frac{3}{4}$ l.

15

Here is a picture of a garden.

Here is a **plan** of the garden.

Each cm on the plan stands for 3 m in the garden.
We say the **scale** of the plan is 1 cm to 3 m
or 1 cm : 3 m.

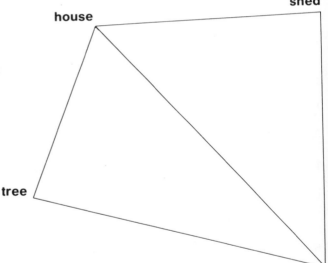

Find the distance in the garden from:

1. the house to the shed
2. the house to the pond
3. the house to the tree
4. the tree to the pond
5. the house to the tree via the pond
6. the house to the pond via the shed
7. the house back to the house via the tree and pond.
8. Find the perimeter of the garden.

Here is a street plan.

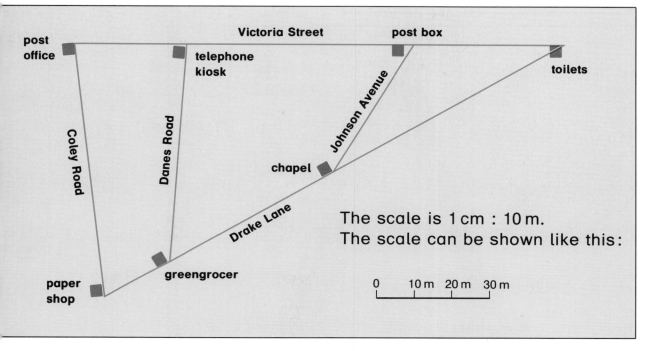

The scale is 1 cm : 10 m.
The scale can be shown like this:

0   10 m 20 m 30 m

1. How long is Victoria Street?

2. How long is Johnson Avenue?

3. How long is Danes Road?

4. How far is it from the paper shop to the telephone kiosk via Danes Road?

5. How far is it from the post office to the greengrocer via Coley Road?

6. How far is it from the telephone kiosk to the chapel via Johnson Avenue?

7. How far is it from the toilets to the paper shop via the telephone kiosk?

8. How much further is it from the paper shop to the telephone kiosk via Coley Road than via Danes Road?

9. Describe the shortest route from the post box to the greengrocer.

10. Describe the shortest route from the post office to the chapel.

Shape and space

16-pin geoboard, spotty paper

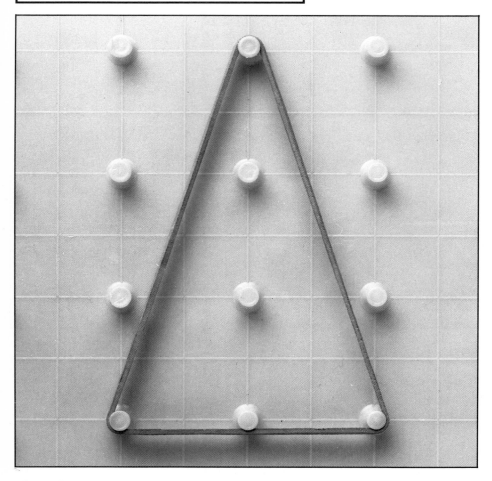

This triangle has 2 equal sides.

Use the glossary to find its name.

How many other triangles with 2 equal sides can you make on your geoboard?

Copy them on spotty paper.

Can you make a triangle with 3 equal sides on your geoboard?

Compasses, ruler

Circle patterns can be drawn in:

a triangle   a hexagon

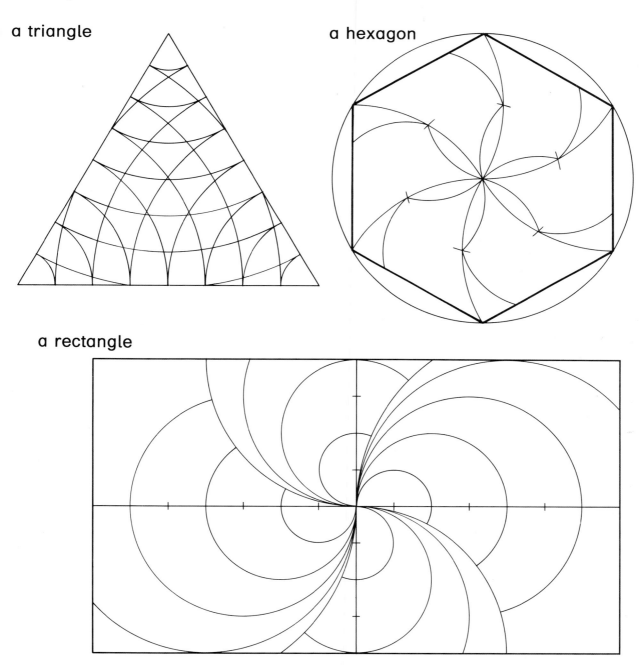

a rectangle

Draw circle patterns of your own.

2 cm squared paper

Draw this on squared paper.

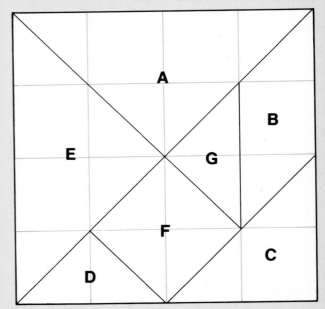

Cut out the 7 shapes.

Which shapes have the same area?

Can you make these shapes?

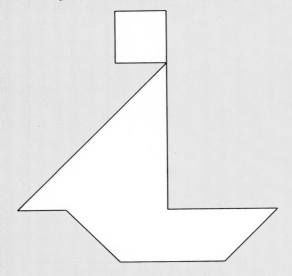

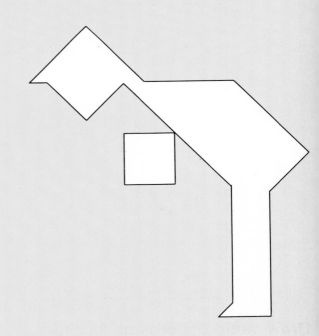

Now try to make a bird.

Take a square of paper
and fold it into quarters.

Cut notches out of the sides.
Do not open the paper.

Draw what you think it will
look like when you open it out.
Now open it to see if you were correct.

Try again with another square of paper.
Cut different notches out of the sides.
Was your drawing more accurate?

How many lines of symmetry has each pattern?

Can you make one like this?

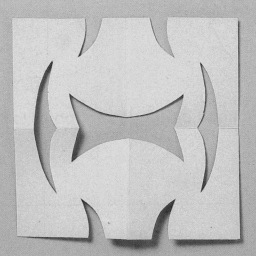

Number and Algebra

Write the fraction shaded.

1.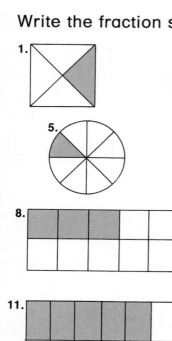

2.

3.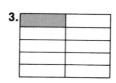

4.

5.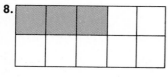

6.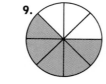

7.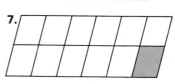

8.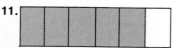

9.

10.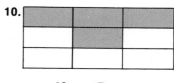

11.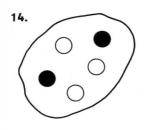

12.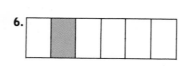

13.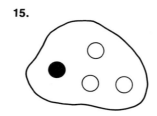

14.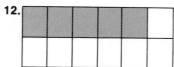

15.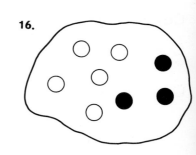

16.

Which fractions do the letters point to?

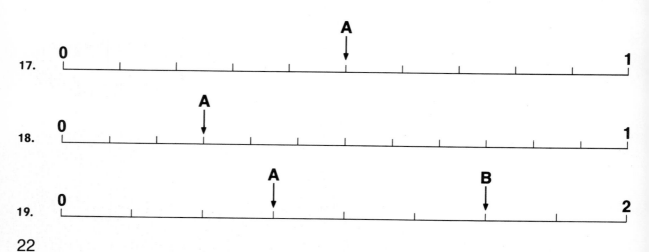

17.

18.

19.

25-pin geoboard, spotty paper

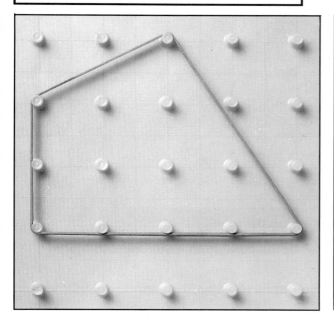 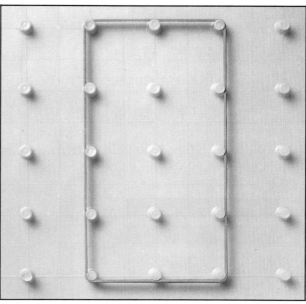

Both these quadrilaterals cover half the geoboard.

Can you make any more shapes that cover half?

Copy them on spotty paper.

Can you make any pentagons that cover half the geoboard?

$\frac{1}{2} = \frac{2}{4}$

$\frac{1}{2}$ is the same as $\frac{2}{4}$.

$\frac{1}{2}$ and $\frac{2}{4}$ are **equivalent fractions**.

Equivalent fractions are worth the same.

Complete these:

1. $\frac{2}{3} = \frac{*}{6}$

2. $\frac{3}{4} = \frac{*}{8}$

3. $\frac{3}{5} = \frac{*}{10}$

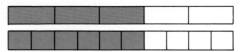

4. $\frac{5}{6} = \frac{*}{12}$

5. $\frac{1}{3} = \frac{*}{9}$

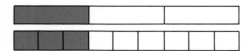

6. $\frac{3}{4} = \frac{*}{12}$

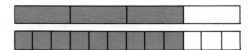

7. $\frac{2}{5} = \frac{*}{10}$

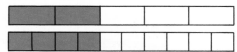

8. $\frac{2}{3} = \frac{*}{9}$

9. $\frac{1}{2} = \frac{*}{6} = \frac{*}{10}$

10. $\frac{1}{4} = \frac{*}{8} = \frac{*}{12}$

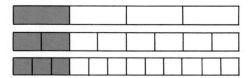

Complete these:

1.

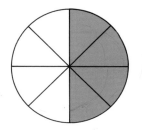

$$\frac{1}{2} = \frac{*4}{8}$$

2.

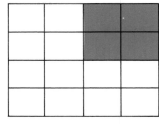

$$\frac{1}{4} = \frac{*}{16}$$

3.

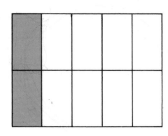

$$\frac{1}{5} = \frac{*}{10}$$

4.

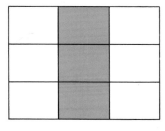

$$\frac{1}{3} = \frac{*}{9}$$

5.

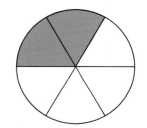

$$\frac{1}{3} = \frac{*}{6}$$

6.

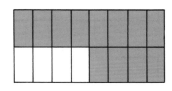

$$\frac{3}{4} = \frac{*}{16}$$

7.

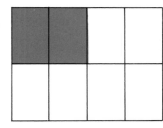

$$\frac{1}{2} = \frac{*}{10}$$

8.

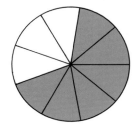

$$\frac{1}{4} = \frac{*}{8}$$

9.

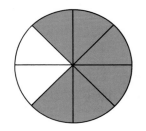

$$\frac{3}{4} = \frac{*}{8}$$

10.

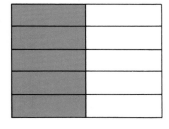

$$\frac{1}{3} = \frac{*}{12}$$

11.

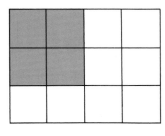

$$\frac{2}{3} = \frac{*}{9}$$

12.

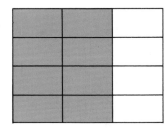

$$\frac{2}{3} = \frac{*}{12}$$

Measures

Find the area of these rectangles.

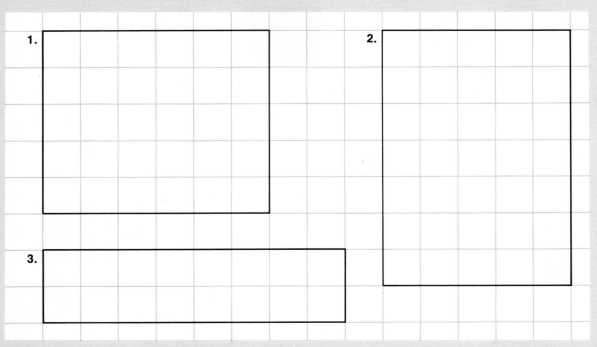

1.

2.

3.

Find a way of calculating the area of the rectangles without counting squares.

Calculate the area of these rectangles.

4.

5.

6.

Calculate the area of these rectangles.

1.

2.

3.

4.

5.

6.

7.

8.

You can find the area of these shapes in different ways.

By addition

Area of large rectangle is	21 cm²
Area of small rectangle is	+ 6 cm²
Area of shape is	27 cm²

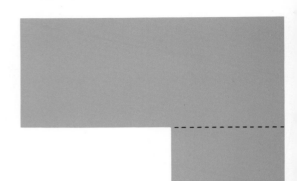

By subtraction

Area of large rectangle is	28 cm²
Area of small rectangle is	− 2 cm²
Area of shape is	26 cm²

Find the area of these shapes.

1.

2.

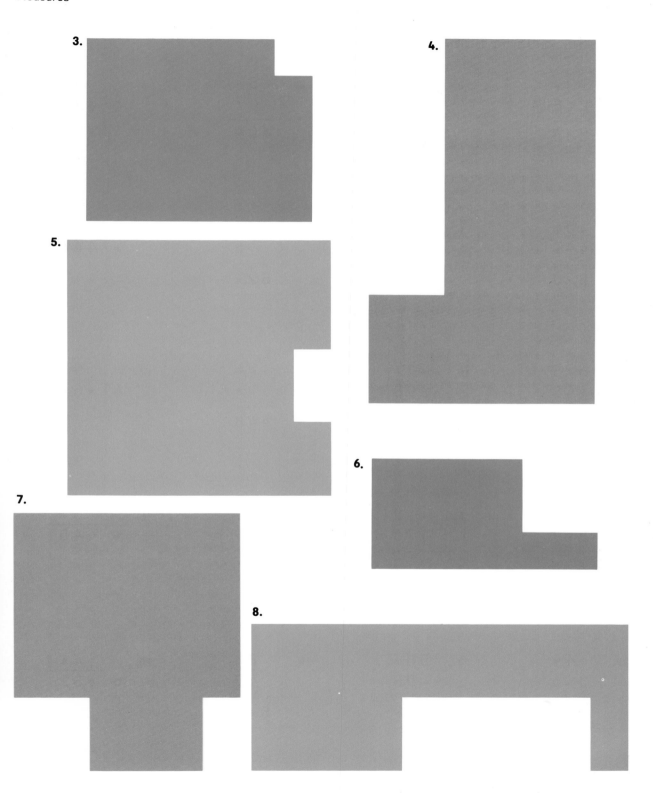

3.

4.

5.

6.

7.

8.

Number and Algebra

Find the missing numbers.

1.
```
  *2*
+ 2*8
------
  385
```

2.
```
  *57
- 18*
-----
  1*8
```

3.
```
   5*
×   7
-----
  4*6
```

4.
```
      49
8)  3*2
```

5.
```
  *06
+ 49*
-----
  8*0
```

6.
```
  2**
- *57
-----
   69
```

7.
```
   *7
×   6
-----
  52*
```

8.
```
      7*
*)  4 4 4
```

9.
```
  5*8
+ *48
-----
  68*
```

10.
```
  *7*
- 298
-----
  1*3
```

11.
```
   *4
×   *
-----
  448
```

12.
```
      91
4)  *6*
```

13.
```
  35*
+ 5*9
-----
  *76
```

14.
```
  **2
- 176
-----
  22*
```

15.
```
   3*
×   9
-----
  3*1
```

16.
```
      5*
*)  4 4 8
```

17.
```
  *49
+ 3*6
-----
  63*
```

18.
```
  50*
- *98
-----
  1*9
```

19.
```
   8*
×   7
-----
  5*1
```

20.
```
      4*
6)  *82
```

To make 0·7 into 7
you multiply by 10.

$$0·7 \xrightarrow{\times 10} 7$$

What has happened in each of these?
It might be addition, subtraction, multiplication or division.

1.

$$0·9 \longrightarrow 1$$

2.

$$1 \longrightarrow 0·8$$

3.

$$17 \longrightarrow 1·7$$

4.

$$0·5 \longrightarrow 50$$

5.

$$0·5 \longrightarrow 1$$

6.

$$2·5 \longrightarrow 1·5$$

7.

$$21 \longrightarrow 2·1$$

8.

$$1·3 \longrightarrow 13$$

9.

$$60 \longrightarrow 0·6$$

10.

$$19 \longrightarrow 190$$

11.

$$400 \longrightarrow 4$$

12.

$$4·3 \longrightarrow 5$$

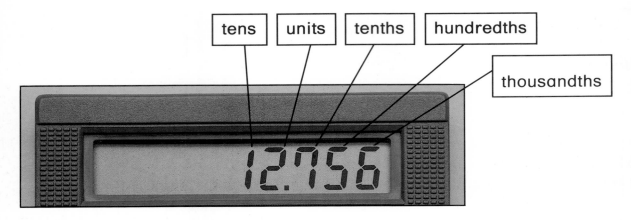

1. What is the digit 5 worth?

2. What do you think the digit 6 is worth?

What is the 7 worth in each of these?

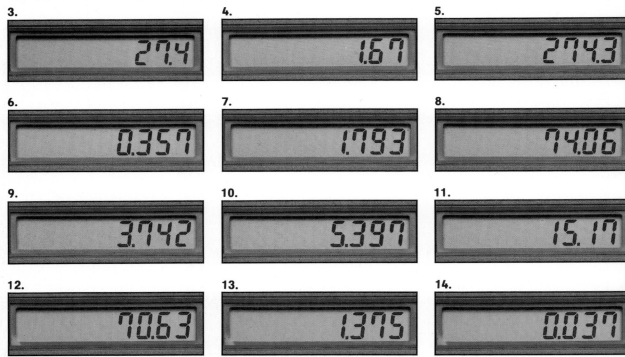

3. 27.4

4. 1.67

5. 274.3

6. 0.357

7. 1.793

8. 74.06

9. 3.742

10. 5.397

11. 15.17

12. 70.63

13. 1.375

14. 0.037

Calculator

What is the input for each of these?

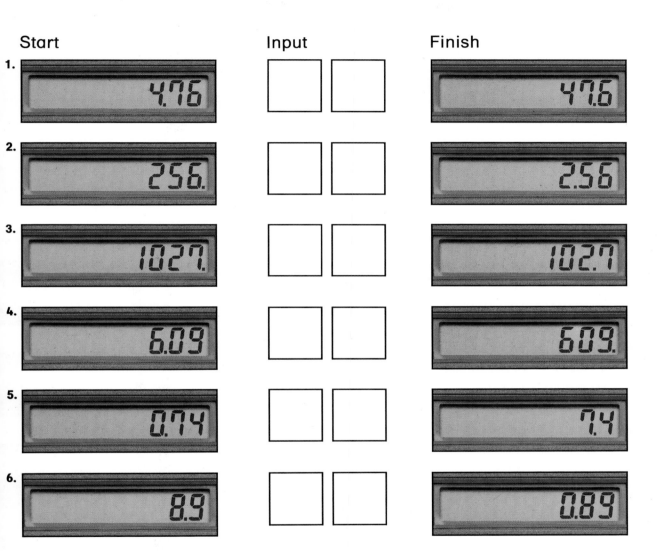

Start	Input	Finish
1. 4.76	☐ ☐	47.6
2. 256.	☐ ☐	2.56
3. 1027.	☐ ☐	102.7
4. 6.09	☐ ☐	609.
5. 0.74	☐ ☐	7.4
6. 8.9	☐ ☐	0.89

Put these numbers in order with the largest first.

7. 1·72, 1·59, 1·6

8. 3·4, 3·19, 3·51

9. 2·99, 3·1, 3·01

10. 5·49, 5·61, 5·5

Measures

A **protractor** measures angles.
Here are two types of protractor.

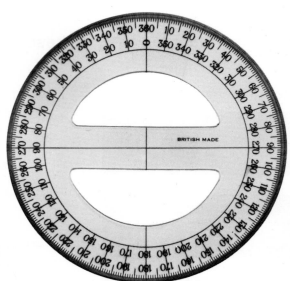

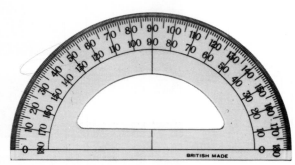

Angles are measured in **degrees**.
There are 90 degrees (90°) in one right angle.

Ask your teacher to show you how to measure these angles.

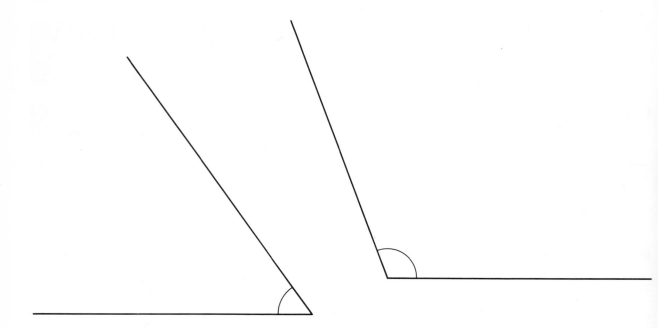

Protractor

Use your protractor to measure these angles.

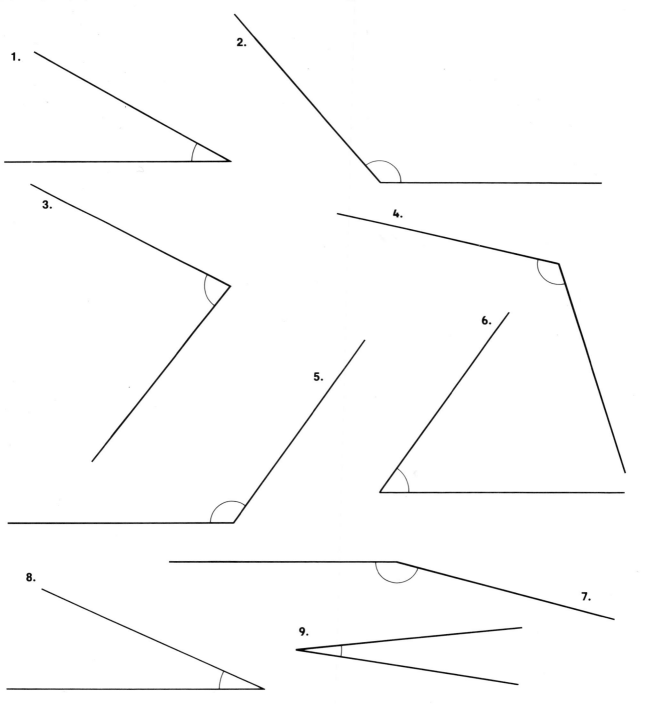

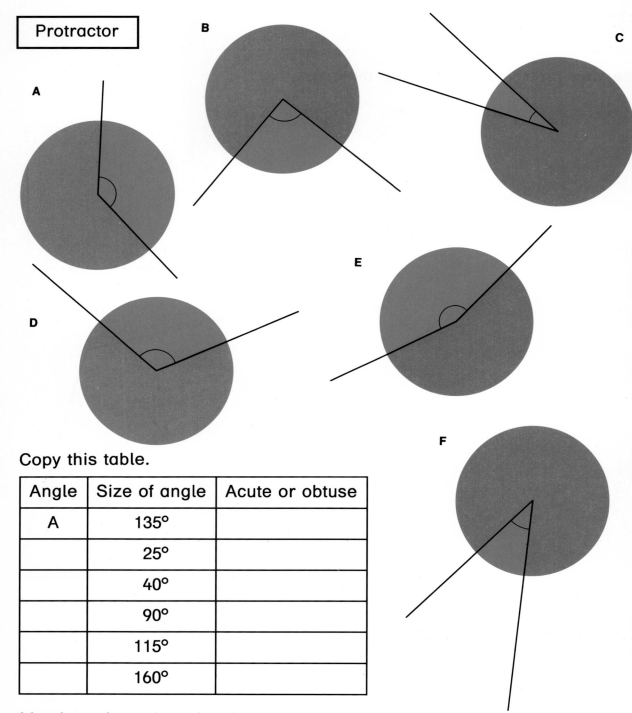

Protractor

A B C

D E

Copy this table.

Angle	Size of angle	Acute or obtuse
A	135°	
	25°	
	40°	
	90°	
	115°	
	160°	

F

Match each angle to its size.
Look up acute and obtuse angles in the glossary.
Write which angles are acute and which are obtuse.

Geostrips

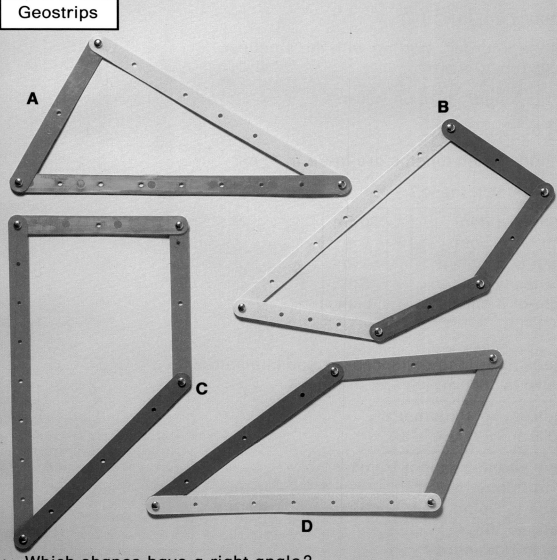

1. Which shapes have a right angle?

2. Which shapes have 2 acute angles?

3. Which shape has 3 obtuse angles?

4. Use geostrips to make a shape which has
   all acute angles
   all right angles
   all obtuse angles.

   Draw the shapes you have made.

37

1. How many cm in $3\frac{1}{2}$ m?

2. Put these in order, starting with the smallest.
   $2\frac{3}{4}$ m, 230 cm, 2·9 m

3. Which is longer, $1\frac{1}{4}$ m or 1·30 m?

4. Find $\frac{1}{2}$ of $1\frac{1}{2}$ m.

5. How many 25 cm lengths are there in $1\frac{1}{4}$ m?

6. Can you match these?

Height of a door	20 cm
Width of a room	2 m
Length of a pencil	1 m
Thickness of a book	5 m
Height of a child	1 cm

When measuring long distances we use kilometres.
A kilometre is 1000 m.

1000 metres	=	1 kilometre
1000 m	=	1 km

How many kilometres is it from:

7. Villy to Pommard?
8. Chablis to Beine?
9. Chablis to Villy?
10. Beine to Pommard?
11. Beine to Villy?
12. Pommard to Chablis?

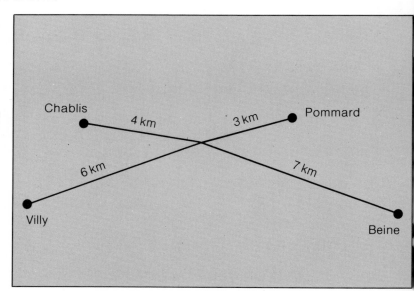

Type of aeroplane	One-eleven	737	Concorde	Jumbo jet
Distance which can be travelled in one hour	866 km	810 km	2400 km	840 km

1. How much further than a 737 will Concorde fly in one hour?

2. How far can a One-eleven fly in 3 hours?

3. How far can a Jumbo jet fly in 6 hours?

4. How far can Concorde fly in $2\frac{1}{2}$ hours?

5. How far can a 737 fly in $1\frac{1}{2}$ hours?

6. How far can a Jumbo jet fly in 20 minutes?

7. How far can a 737 fly in 40 minutes?

Tape measure, squared paper

1. Measure the heights of 6 friends.
   Measure their waists.
   Record your results in a table.

Name	Height	Waist

2. Draw a column graph of your results like this:

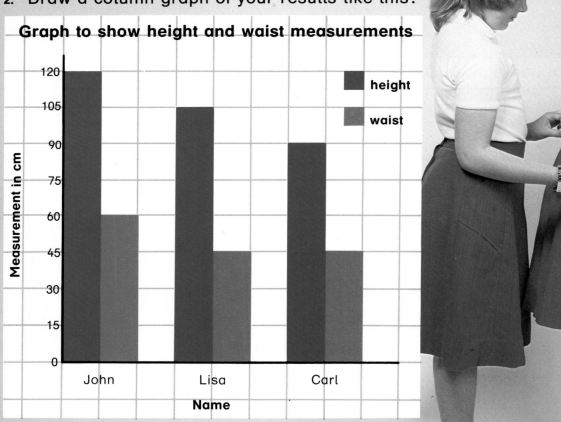

Graph to show height and waist measurements

3. Approximately how many times does each waist measurement fit into the height measurement?

Hollow 10 cm cube, scales, sand, peas

1. Weigh the hollow 10 cm cube.
   Record its weight.

   Fill the cube with peas and weigh it.
   Record its weight.
   Use your results to find the weight of the peas.

   Fill the cube with sand.
   Find the weight of the sand.

   Fill the cube with water.
   Find the weight of the water.

2. Which weighed most, the peas, the sand or the water?

3. What was the difference in weight between the peas and the water?

4. What was the difference in weight between the sand and the water?

5. What was the difference in weight between the sand and the peas?

6. What do you notice about the weight of the water?

Handling data

This graph is called a **stick graph**.

Instead of drawing columns to show the information, straight lines are used.

1. What is the depth of the Red Sea?

2. What is the depth of the English Channel?

3. Which seas are deeper than the Irish Sea?

4. Can you find the name of a sea that is deeper than the Black Sea?

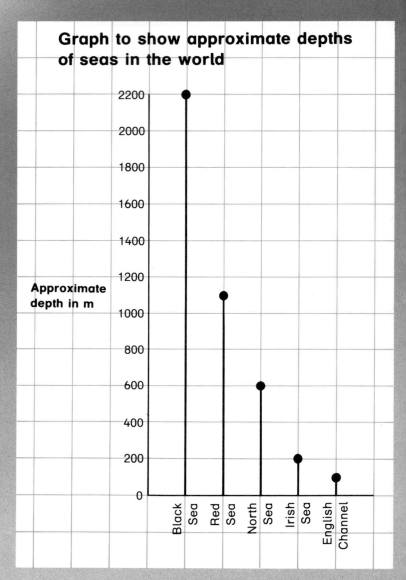

Graph to show approximate depths of seas in the world

Approximate depth in m

This map shows seven rivers in England and Wales.

1. Draw a stick graph to show their lengths.

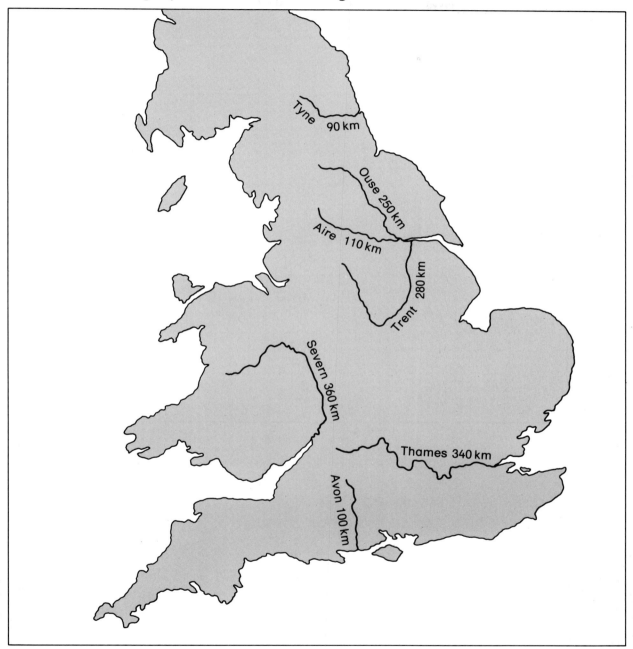

2. Which of the rivers is nearest your home?

3. Which is the longest river in the world?

The numbers shown on the two axes are called **co-ordinates**.
Co-ordinates help you to plot points on a graph.
The co-ordinate on the horizontal axis is always written before
the co-ordinate on the vertical axis.

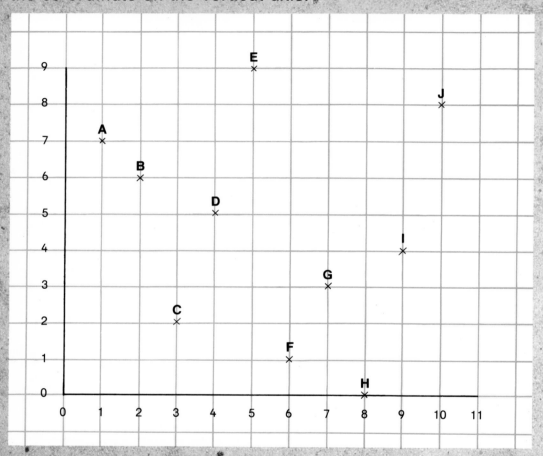

The co-ordinates of Point A are (1,7).
Write the co-ordinates of all the other points.

Draw a horizontal axis and label it 0 to 9.
Draw a vertical axis and label it 0 to 5.
Join up these points in order: (1,4) (2,5) (3,4) (2,3) (1,4)
Now join up these points in order: (3,4) (8,4) (9,3) (9,2) (8,3) (8,0)
(7,0) (7,2) (4,2) (4,0) (3,0) (3,4)

Make up some designs yourself for a friend to plot.

This old map was found in a sailor's chest.
It is a map of a treasure island.
The clues on it explain where the treasure is buried.
Can you find the treasure?

Copy the map on squared paper.
Find the place where
the treasure is hidden.
Write its co-ordinates.

TREASURE CLUES
Plot the co-ordinates (3,2) and (6,8).
Join them with a straight line.
Plot the co-ordinates (2,8) and (11,2).
Join them with a straight line.
The treasure is hidden where
the lines cross.

Number and Algebra

Squared paper

When two numbers are multiplied the answer is called the **product**.

Find the product of these numbers.

1. 93 and 7
2. 128 and 9
3. 6 and 143
4. 810 and 10
5. 5 and 964
6. 203 and 8

7. Write down all the numbers that divide exactly into 24.

8. Which numbers will divide exactly into both 36 and 48?

9. Which numbers under 30 can be divided exactly by both 2 and 3?

10. Which numbers under 50 have a remainder of 4 when divided by 5?

11. Copy this on squared paper.

91									82
		56						50	
			30						
	59		13			10			
				3	2			47	
				4	1				
		35		5	6	7			
							21		
					40			43	
100	65								73

Write these numbers on the grid: 37, 75, 24, 53.

Write all the square numbers on the grid.
What do you notice about them?

Calculator

Put consecutive numbers in the boxes.

1. $\boxed{39} = \boxed{} + \boxed{}$

2. $\boxed{157} = \boxed{} + \boxed{}$

3. $\boxed{21} = \boxed{} + \boxed{} + \boxed{}$

4. $\boxed{144} = \boxed{} + \boxed{} + \boxed{}$

5. $\boxed{122} = \boxed{} + \boxed{} + \boxed{} + \boxed{}$

6. $\boxed{306} = \boxed{} \times \boxed{}$

7. $\boxed{210} = \boxed{} \times \boxed{}$

8. $\boxed{552} = \boxed{} \times \boxed{}$

9. $\boxed{812} = \boxed{} \times \boxed{}$

10. $\boxed{504} = \boxed{} \times \boxed{} \times \boxed{}$

11. $\boxed{990} = \boxed{} \times \boxed{} \times \boxed{}$

12. $\boxed{210} = \boxed{} \times \boxed{} \times \boxed{}$

13. $\boxed{720} = \boxed{} \times \boxed{} \times \boxed{}$

The Tudor kings and queens

Henry VII
1485–1509

Henry VIII
1509–1547

Edward VI
1547–1553

Mary I
1553–1558

Elizabeth I
1558–1603

The Stuart kings and queens

James I
1603–1625

Charles I
1625–1649

Charles II
1660–1685

James II
1685–1688

William III and Mary
1688–1702

Anne
1702–1?

1. Which monarch ruled for the longest time?

2. How long did the Tudors rule?

3. Which monarch ruled for the shortest time?

4. Which monarchs ruled for 24 years?

5. Which monarch ruled for 17 years longer than Mary I?

6. How many years passed between the deaths of Mary I and James II?

7. For how long was there no monarch on the throne?

8. How long did the Stuarts rule?

Look for information about Roman numbers in an encyclopaedia.

Marcus

his father

his grandfather

1. Marcus is XI years old.
   His father is XLIV years old.
   His grandfather is LXXXVI years old.
   Write their ages in our number system.

What do these numbers say?

2.

3.

4.

5.

6.

7.

8.
CHAPTER XLIII

1. Using 4s

What other numbers can you make from four 4s?

$44 + 4 + 4 = 52$

$\frac{4}{4} + 4 - 4 = 1$

2. Making 100

Put these numbers into sets.
Each set must total 100.

35

49

17

41

24

58

14

37

25

1. Use the digits 1 to 9.
   Arrange them on the grid.
   Find each row total.
   Find each column total.

   Rearrange the digits to make as many odd totals as you can.

2. Arrange the digits 0 to 9 to fit in the boxes.

□ > □ > □ < □ < □ > □ > □ < □ < □ > □

Measures

Look at a current calendar.

1. How many months are there in a year?

2. Write the names of the months that have 31 days.

3. Write the names of the months that have 30 days.

4. Write the name of the month which has 28 or 29 days.

5. How many weeks in a year?

6. How many days in a year?

7. How many Mondays in March?

8. John's birthday is on June 12th.
   Peter's birthday is on July 3rd.
   How many weeks between their birthdays?

9. Sports meetings are held on each Saturday in June, July and August.
   How many sports meetings are held?

10. Susan has to run in the school sports held on August 23rd.
    She wants to train for five weeks before the sports.
    On what date must she start training?

11. Paul is a good sprinter. He will run in his school sports on June 17th.
    The next time he will run will be at the county sports on July 12th.
    How many days are there between the two meetings?

Stop-watch, trundle wheel

Hour hand

Minute hand

This hand measures seconds.
It is called the **second hand**.

The second hand takes **1 minute** to go once round the face.
The second hand takes **60 seconds** to go once round the face.

60 seconds = 1 minute
60 sec = 1 min

Write the number of seconds in:

1. 3 min
2. $1\frac{1}{2}$ min
3. 2 min
4. $2\frac{1}{2}$ min

5. 2 min 15 sec
6. 1 min 40 sec
7. 1 min 25 sec
8. $1\frac{3}{4}$ min

9. Ask your teacher to show you how to use a stop-watch.
Estimate how long it will take you to write this sentence:
'The stop-watch is an instrument for measuring time very accurately.'
Now copy the sentence and time yourself.
Write how long it took you.

10. How far can you walk in 10 sec?
Estimate first, then time yourself. Record your result.

11. Now find out how far you can run, hop, skip and jump in 10 sec.
Draw a column graph to show your results.

This table shows the cost of posting parcels in 1988.

Weight not over	First class	Second class
500 g	92p	70p
600 g	£1·15	85p
700 g	£1·35	£1·00
750 g	£1·45	£1·05
800 g	£1·55	Not admissible over 750 g
900 g	£1·70	
1000 g	£1·85	
Each extra 250 g or part thereof 45p		

1. What would it cost to send each of these by first class post?

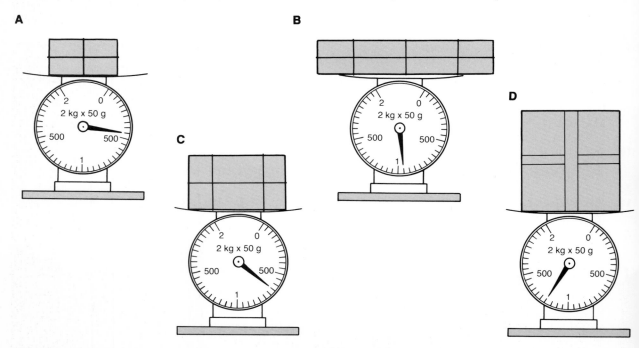

2. Which of the parcels could be sent by second class post?
3. How much would each one cost?

54

Which is the better buy and how much would be saved?

1.

2.

Centimetre cubes

1. Each of these cuboids is made from 12 cubes.

Make cuboids from 18 cubes.
How many different ones can you make?

2. How many cubes
are there in
this cuboid?

Make some more cuboids
with the same number
of cubes.

How many cubes in each of these?

Number and Algebra

Find the missing numbers.

1.
```
    4 2 *
      7 8
  + * 9 2
  ───────
    6 * 5
```

2.
```
    2 * 4
    4 8 *
  +   6 9
  ───────
    * 6 0
```

3.
```
      8 5
    5 * 4
  + * 0 *
  ───────
    7 8 6
```

4.
```
    4 2 *
  - * * 7
  ───────
    2 3 6
```

5.
```
    * * 2
  - 4 1 3
  ───────
    1 8 *
```

6.
```
    * 2 *
  - 3 * 3
  ───────
    1 6 1
```

7.
```
    * * 8
  ×     7
  ───────
    2 9 9 *
```

8.
```
    3 * 9
  ×     *
  ───────
    2 * 7 2
```

9.
```
    * 6 3
  ×     4
  ───────
    2 2 * 2
```

10.
```
        6 * 4
      ─────────
  6 ) * 1 0 *
```

11.
```
        3 * 9
      ─────────
  * ) 1 6 4 *
```

12.
```
        * * 8
      ─────────
  9 ) 1 7 8 *
```

13.
```
    3 4 *
    1 2 8
  + * 3 4
  ───────
    1 1 * 9
```

14.
```
    3 7 * 4
  - 1 9 2 *
  ─────────
    * 7 7 8
```

15.
```
    3 6 *
  ×     8
  ───────
    * 9 * 6
```

16.
```
        4 7 *
      ─────────
  7 ) 3 * 0 4
```

17.
```
    * 5 8
  ×     *
  ───────
    * 8 3 2
```

18.
```
        7 2 *
      ─────────
  * ) 4 3 4 4
```

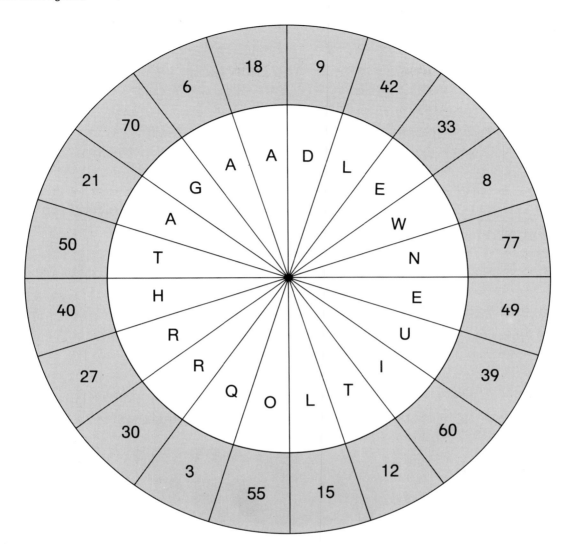

1. Find the numbers on the wheel which are multiples of 3.
   Write the matching letters.
   Rearrange the letters to make the name of a shape.

2. Now find all the multiples of 4.
   Write and rearrange the letters to make a word.

3. Do the same with the multiples of 11, then 10 and then 7.

4. Now draw what the five words say.

Calculator

It is sometimes necessary to count the number of vehicles that use a road each day.
This is called a traffic census.
A traffic census was taken on a busy road near London.
This table shows how many vehicles used the road on the day of the census.

	Cars	Vans	Buses	Lorries	Motor cycles
To London	1825	729	136	1001	124
From London	2136	802	172	763	96

1. How many cars used the road that day?

2. How many more cars than lorries were counted?

3. How many more cars were travelling away from London than to London?

4. How many more cars than vans passed the census point?

5. How many vehicles were travelling to London on that road that day?

1. Find as many ways as you can of scoring 46 with 3 darts.

2. How would these balls have to be rearranged so that each line of three numbers adds up to the same total?

3. How would these cards have to be rearranged so that each line of three numbers adds up to the same total?

1. These table facts give an answer of 36.

   4 × 9   6 × 6   9 × 4

   Which table facts give answers of   24   18   30

2. Find the missing numbers.

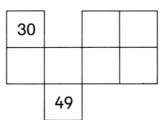

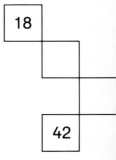

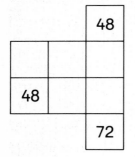

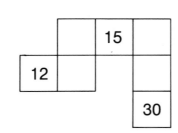

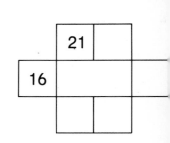

3. Find the missing numbers.

$$6 \overline{)\square\square} \quad 8 \text{ r } 2$$

$$\square \overline{)6\,8} \quad 9 \text{ r } \square$$

$$9 \overline{)5\,2} \quad \square \text{ r } 7$$

$$8 \overline{)\square\square} \quad 7 \text{ r } 6$$

$$3 \overline{)2\,9} \quad \square \text{ r } 2$$

$$4 \overline{)3\,5} \quad 8 \text{ r } \square$$

$$7 \overline{)\square\square} \quad 7 \text{ r } 4$$

$$\square \overline{)3\,9} \quad 4 \text{ r } 7$$

$$5 \overline{)4\,7} \quad \square \text{ r } 2$$

Calculator

You can only use the keys shown.
Find a way of doing each of these.

1.
```
  124
+  35
_____

_____
```

2.
```
   42
-  15
_____

_____
```

3.
```
  272
×    5
_____

_____
```

4.
```
  83
+ 96
_____

_____
```

5.
```
   52
-  23
_____

_____
```

6.
```
  256
×    3
_____

_____
```

7.
```
  29
+ 67
_____

_____
```

8.
```
   94
-  27
_____

_____
```

9.
```
   76
×   7
_____

_____
```

Assessment

1. $5278 + 1036 + 976$

2. $1\frac{1}{4}$ kg $\times$ 6

3. Find the product of 8 and 137.

4. Find the area of this shape.

5. What does this reading show?

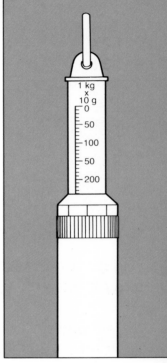

6. These are triangular numbers. Write the next two numbers.

   1, 3, 6, 10, ____, ____

7. Change 2 min 40 sec to seconds.

8. Change 135 sec to minutes and seconds.

9. Put these in order, beginning with the smallest.
   (a) $1\frac{3}{4}$ kg, 1·700 kg, 1500 g
   (b) 2·400 l, 2600 ml, $2\frac{1}{2}$ l

10.
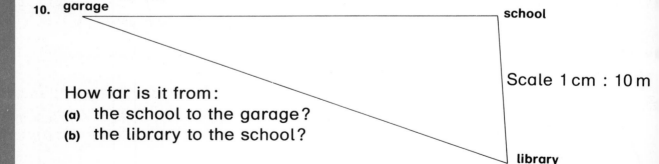

    How far is it from:
    (a) the school to the garage?
    (b) the library to the school?

    Scale 1 cm : 10 m

11. Find the value of the missing numbers.

(a) $\dfrac{2}{5} = \dfrac{\square}{10}$

(b) $\dfrac{\square}{4} = \dfrac{2}{8}$

12. Make these numbers 10 times smaller.

(a) 2·7

(b) 36

(c) 14·8

13. Measure these angles.

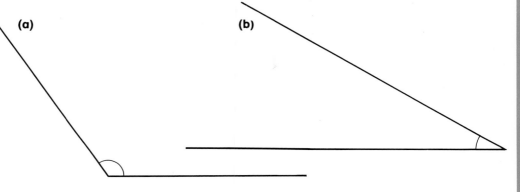

(a)

(b)

14. Which numbers will divide exactly into both 18 and 21?

16. Three bottles each hold 750 ml. How much do they hold altogether?

15. Put in the missing sign, > or <.

3·5 ☐ 3·45

2·65 ☐ 2·7

1·75 ☐ 1·09

17. 3004 − 616

19. 7) 3 8 4 3

20.
```
   1 3 8
 ×     7
 _____

 _____
```

18. Write the co-ordinates of each point.

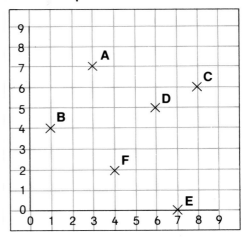

Multiple choice

Choose the correct answer.

1. 1 metre is
   (a) 10 cm
   (b) 100 cm
   (c) 1000 cm

2. 1 kilogram is
   (a) 10 g
   (b) 100 g
   (c) 1000 g

3. The perimeter of a
   4 cm square is
   (a) 16 cm
   (b) 16 cm²
   (c) 8 cm

4. Add $\frac{3}{4}$ to $\frac{3}{4}$.
   (a) $\frac{6}{8}$
   (b) $1\frac{1}{2}$
   (c) $\frac{3}{8}$

5. 1 more than 2099
   (a) 3000
   (b) 2090
   (c) 2100

6. 1 less than 2000
   (a) 1999
   (b) 1099
   (c) 999

7. The difference between
   450 ml and 1 litre
   (a) 1450 ml
   (b) 650 ml
   (c) 550 ml

8. The total of
   70 cm, 35 cm and 45 cm
   (a) 1·50 m
   (b) 150 mm
   (c) 1·50 cm

9. Multiply 3·5 by 10.
   (a) 35
   (b) 3·50
   (c) 0·35

10. Divide 3·5 by 10
    (a) 35
    (b) 3·50
    (c) 0·35

11. 1 min 45 sec is
    (a) 115 sec
    (b) 95 sec
    (c) 105 sec

12. $2\frac{1}{4}$ kg is the same as
    (a) 2400 g
    (b) 2250 g
    (c) 2200 g

Number and Algebra

Add 1 to each of these numbers.

1. 409
2. 359
3. 799
4. 989
5. 1999

Subtract 1 from each of these numbers.

6. 320
7. 400
8. 990
9. 4000
10. 6100

Write these as figures.

11. Four thousand and nine
12. Six thousand and seventeen
13. One thousand and one
14. One thousand, one hundred

Multiply each of these by 10.

15. 14
16. 73
17. 100
18. 123
19. 403

Divide each of these by 10.

20. 70
21. 110
22. 570
23. 1000
24. 3040

Using the digits 2, 4 and 5

25. make the largest number
26. make a number exactly divisible by 7
27. make the smallest even number
28. make the largest multiple of 5.

Using the digits 2, 3 and 4

29. make the smallest even number
30. make a number exactly divisible by 8
31. make the largest number
32. make the number nearest to 330.

This table shows the number of visitors to Beaulieu Museum one week.

Sun	Mon	Tue	Wed	Thur	Fri	Sat
162	120	132	74	102	136	212

1. What was the total number of visitors that week?

2. If the visitors had been spread equally over the week, how many would there have been each day?

You have found the **average** number of visitors each day.

To find an average, total the groups
and then divide by the number of groups.

Find the average of these:

3. 72, 46, 89, 112, 101

4. £15, £9, £8, £12, £6

5. 5 m, 7 m, 12 m, 8 m

6. 12 kg, 6 kg, 15 kg, 9 kg, 3 kg

7. 8 l, 5 l, 11 l, 4 l

Some visitors went to the souvenir shop.

1. Mrs. Mills liked the tea towels.
   She decided to buy 6 of them.
   How much did they cost her?

2. Mrs. Johnson wanted to buy presents for her friends.
   She bought 8 beakers and 6 pens.
   How much did she pay?

3. Mr. Adams owned a café.
   He wanted to buy 90 beakers.
   He was charged a special price of £5·80 for 10.
   How much did he pay?

4. Mrs. Selby bought 4 of each item in the shop.
   How much did she pay?

Number problems

$(4 \times 3) - 2 = 10$

When part of a number problem is inside brackets you must work that part out first.

$(4 \times 3) - 2 = 10$
$12 - 2 = 10$

$(16 - 4) - (4 + 3) = 5$
$12 - 7 = 5$

Find where to put the brackets in these problems.

1. $8 + 6 \times 2 = 28$

2. $15 - 3 + 4 = 8$

3. $20 + 12 \div 3 = 24$

4. $13 - 1 \div 4 = 3$

5. $5 + 3 \times 4 = 32$

6. $9 - 2 \times 0 = 9$

7. $6 \times 5 - 3 = 27$

8. $4 \div 4 \times 0 = 0$

9. $19 - 3 \times 5 = 4$

10. $7 + 8 \div 8 = 8$

11. $10 + 2 \times 6 - 4 = 18$

12. $36 - 16 \div 4 + 8 = 40$

13. $12 + 4 \div 24 \div 3 = 2$

14. $9 \times 8 + 4 \times 7 = 100$

15. $7 + 1 \div 3 + 5 = 1$

16. $2 \times 6 - 4 + 4 = 4$

17. $18 + 3 - 7 \div 7 = 2$

18. $6 \times 3 \div 9 \times 0 = 0$

19. Make up a number problem to give an answer of 1.

You can only use the digits 1, 2, 3 and 4.
All the four digits must be used.
You can only use each digit once.
You may use any of the signs $+ - \times \div$.
You may use brackets.

One way is like this: $(3 + 2) - (4 \times 1)$
Find another way.

20. Using the same rules as the last question, make up number problems to give answers from 2 to 12.

Divide these numbers by 10.

1. 460   2. 610   3. 4800   4. 2620   5. 7460   6. 3270

There is no remainder.
We say the numbers are **exactly divisible** by 10.
Write the rule which tells you that a number is exactly divisible by 10.

Which of these numbers are exactly divisible by 5?

7. 495, 366, 2740, 3775, 4163, 5360

Write the rule which tells you that a number is exactly divisible by 5.

Which of these numbers are exactly divisible by 4?

8. 736, 612, 331, 1540, 7322, 3016

Look carefully at the last two digits of the numbers.
Write the rule which tells you that a number is exactly divisible by 4.

9. Leap year dates are divisible by 4.
Use the rule to find out which of these events happened in a leap year.

1431
Joan of Arc
burnt at the stake

1564
William Shakespeare
born

1666
Great Fire of London

1776
American Declaration of
Independence from Britain

1840
Penny postage
introduced

1953
Coronation of
Queen Elizabeth II

Measures

Balance (or scales), marbles, measuring jug, sand

Find the weight of 750 ml of water.
Remember to weigh the empty container first.
Calculate the weight of $1\frac{1}{2}$ l of water.

Weigh a litre of sand.
Calculate the weight of a 10 l bucket
full of sand.

Weigh 10 marbles.
Calculate the weight of 1 marble.
Calculate the weight of 100 marbles.

How many marbles weigh 50 g?
Calculate how many marbles there are in 500 g.
Calculate how many marbles there are in 1 kg.

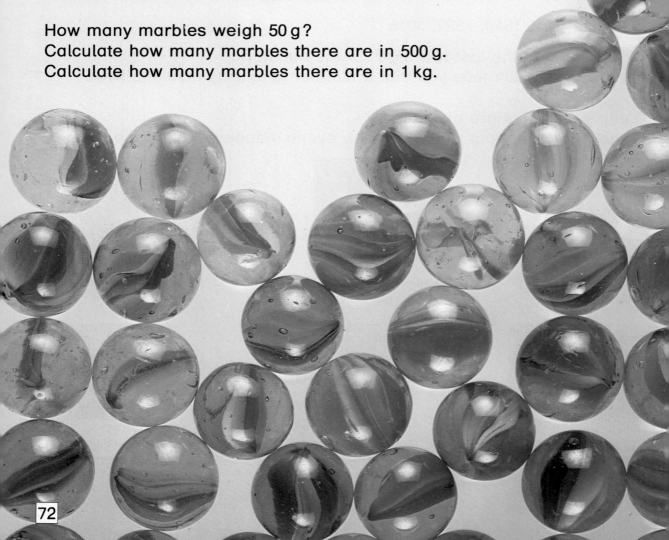

Which is the best buy?

1.

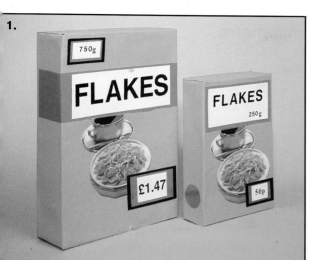

2.

3.

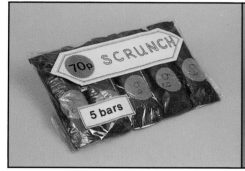

4.

When measuring lines exactly we need a smaller measurement than the centimetre.
This smaller measurement is called a **millimetre**.

10 millimetres = 1 centimetre
10 **mm** = 1 cm

This line measures 8 cm 2 mm.

_____

Measure these lines.

1. _____   **2.** _____

3. _____

8 cm 2 mm can be written as 8·2 cm or 82 mm.

4. Measure these lines.
   Record your measurements in a table.

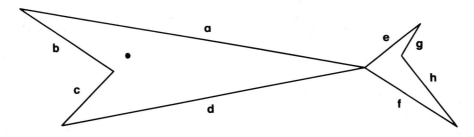

line a	9 cm 3 mm	9·3 cm	93 mm
b			
c			
d			
e			
f			
g			
h			

cm squared paper

1. Measure these lines.
   Write your answers in mm.

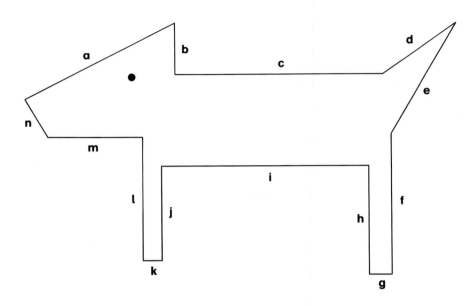

Draw these lines.

2. 84 mm   3. 6·3 cm   4. 9·7 cm   5. 107 mm   6. 119 mm

7. 12·3 cm   8. 7·5 cm   9. 48 mm   10. 51 mm   11. 38 mm

12. On cm squared paper draw a 2 cm square.
    Measure the length of its diagonal in mm.
    Do the same for squares with the sizes shown in the table below.
    Draw the table and record your results.

Size of square	Length of diagonal
2 cm	
3 cm	
4 cm	
6 cm	
8 cm	

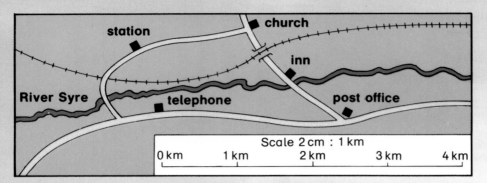

1. How far is it from the church to the inn?

2. How far is it from the station to the post office via the church?

3. How far is it from the inn to the telephone via the post office?

4. How far is it from the post office to where the railway passes over the road?

5. How much further is it from the church to the telephone via the post office than via the station?

This chart shows the distance in
miles between the towns.
The coloured square shows that Leeds
and Liverpool are 75 miles apart.

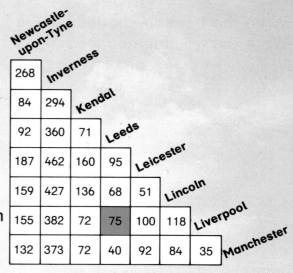

Newcastle-upon-Tyne	Inverness	Kendal	Leeds	Leicester	Lincoln	Liverpool	Manchester
268							
84	294						
92	360	71					
187	462	160	95				
159	427	136	68	51			
155	382	72	75	100	118		
132	373	72	40	92	84	35	

1. How far is it from Manchester
   to Inverness?

2. How far is it from Kendal to
   Newcastle-upon-Tyne?

3. I travel from Leeds to Leicester, then
   on to Lincoln. How far have I gone?

Here is a map showing
the distances in kilometres
between five towns.

4. Copy and complete this chart
   showing the shortest distances
   between the towns.

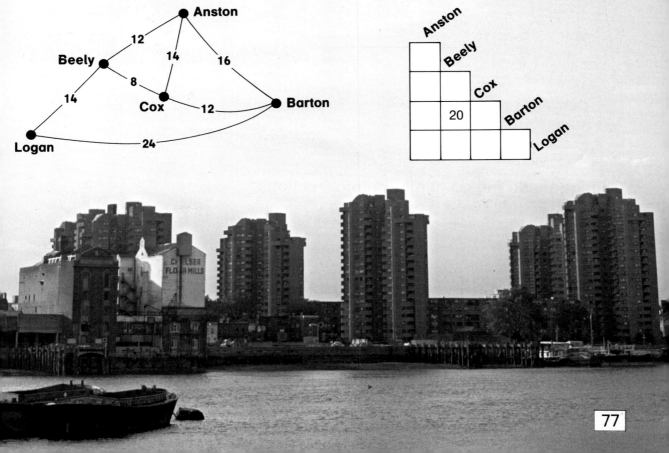

Number and Algebra

Write the fraction shaded.
Write the fraction not shaded.

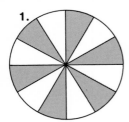
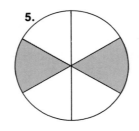
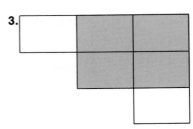

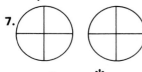
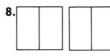
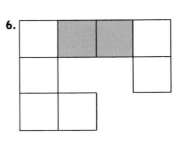

Complete these.

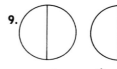

7. $2 = \dfrac{*}{4}$

8. $2 = \dfrac{*}{2}$

9. $1\frac{1}{2} = \dfrac{*}{2}$

10. $2\frac{1}{4} = \dfrac{*}{4}$

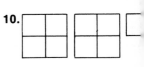

> A number that has whole ones and a fraction is called
> a **mixed number**.
>
> $1\frac{3}{4}$ is a mixed number.

Change these mixed numbers into fractions.

11. $4\frac{1}{2}$ 12. $2\frac{3}{8}$ 13. $2\frac{3}{10}$ 14. $1\frac{3}{4}$ 15. $1\frac{7}{10}$

Change these fractions into mixed numbers.

16. $\frac{7}{4}$ 17. $\frac{7}{2}$ 18. $\frac{19}{10}$ 19. $\frac{21}{8}$ 20. $\frac{27}{8}$

25-pin geoboard, spotty paper

Halve your geoboard by stretching an elastic band
from one side to the other.
The same number of pins must be on each side of the band.

How many different ways can you find of halving the board?
Record your results on spotty paper.

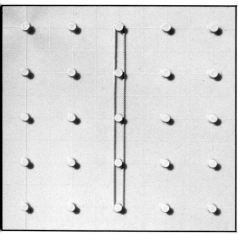 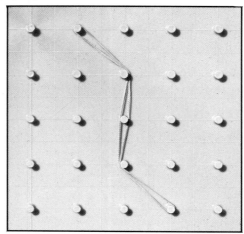

Quarter your geoboard by stretching two elastic bands
across the board.

How many different ways can you find of quartering the board?
Record your results on spotty paper.

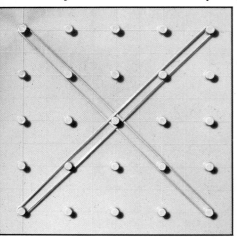 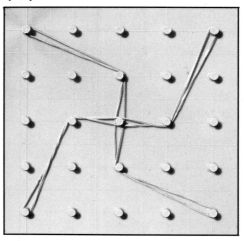

Plane shapes

1. This is half of a shape.

The whole shape could be any of these.

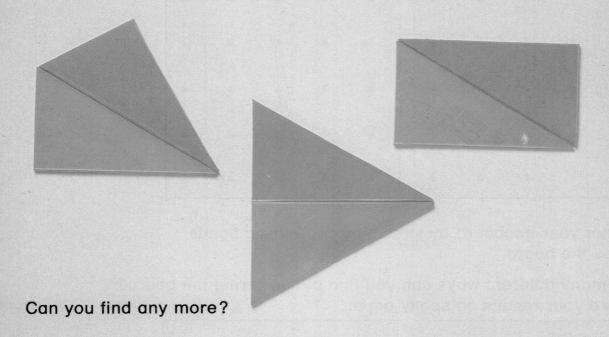

Can you find any more?

2. This is half of a shape.

   Draw as many different
   whole shapes as you can.

Plane shapes

This is a quarter of a shape.

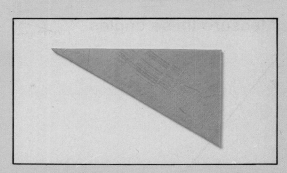

1. Could the whole shape be a triangle?

2. How many different quadrilaterals could the whole shape be?

3. What is the largest number of sides the whole shape could have?

Experiment with other shapes which are quarters.

Measures

Measure these angles.

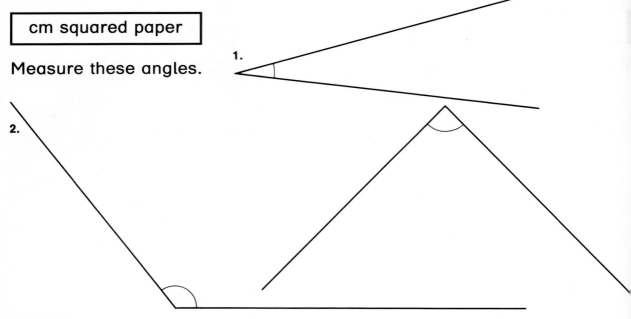

1.

2.

Draw these angles.

4. 79°   **5.** 108°   **6.** 171°   **7.** 16°   **8.** 42°

Write beside each angle whether it is acute or obtuse.

On squared paper draw the axes and label them as shown.

9. Join up these co-ordinates.
   (8,1) (2,2) (5,9)
Measure the angle and give its name.

Now do the same for these:

10. (9,2) (4,1) (1,6)
11. (1,4) (6,8) (5,1)
12. (1,8) (8,5) (6,1)
13. (4,1) (2,8) (7,2)

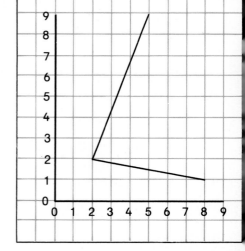

14. On squared paper label axes 0 to 7.
   Draw the triangle whose co-ordinates are (1,1) (3,6) (6,2).
   Measure each angle.

Plain paper, scissors

1. Draw a triangle on paper.
   Cut it out.

Rip off the three corners.

Fit the corners together.

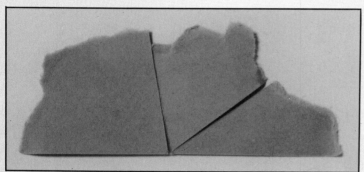

Repeat this with different types of triangle.
What do you notice about the three angles of a triangle?

2. Draw different quadrilaterals.

Rip off the corners.

Fit them together.

What do you notice about the four angles
of a quadrilateral?

Shape and space

Plane shapes, scissors, paper

Use the glossary to help you.

1. Cut out a paper circle.
   Make a line of symmetry on the circle.
   What is half a circle called?

2. Make six other lines of symmetry.
   What could each line of symmetry
   be called?

3. Find as many different quadrilaterals as you can.

(a) Which quadrilaterals have both diagonals as lines of symmetry?

(b) Which quadrilaterals have only one diagonal as a line of symmetry?

(c) Which quadrilaterals have neither diagonal as a line of symmetry?

(d) Which quadrilaterals have lines of symmetry but not along diagonals?

Plane shapes

Are you a good sorter?

1. Find a set of shapes where the diagonals halve the shape.

2. Find a set of shapes where the diagonals cross at right angles.

3. Find a set of shapes where the diagonals cut each other in half.

4. Find a set of shapes where the diagonals cut the corner angles in half.

What other ways can you find of sorting the shapes?

Paper circle, string, tin lid

Find the centre of the paper circle by folding.
Mark the centre with a coloured pencil.
How do you know the mark is the centre?
Measure the lines you have made.

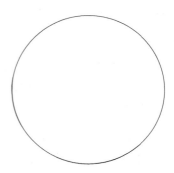

The distance from the edge of the circle to the centre is called the **radius**.

The word for more than one radius is **radii**.

The perimeter of a circle is called its **circumference**.

Stick your paper circle in your book.
Label the circumference, radius and diameter.

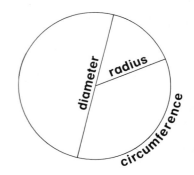

Find a tin lid.
Use string to measure its circumference.

Measure the circumference of
other circular objects.

Compasses

Before using the compasses,
make sure that the pencil point
and compass point are level.

Open the compasses to 4 cm.
Draw a circle using the compasses.

Draw circles that have radii
of 5 cm, 7 cm and 3 cm.

Now use the compasses to draw circle patterns.

87

General

Strips of paper

Make a hoop with a paper strip.

If you cut along the centre of the strip what
will happen?
See if you were correct.

Make another hoop but put a twist in the
paper first.
What will happen if you cut along the centre of
the strip?
See if you were correct.

Put two twists in a hoop and repeat what you
have been doing.

4 red counters, 4 yellow counters

Put 4 red counters on the top row.
Put 4 yellow counters on the bottom row.

You have to change the positions of the red and yellow counters.
The counters can only slide into empty spaces.
They cannot jump over each other.

Number and Algebra

Make these numbers 10 times larger.

1. 56
2. 40
3. 71
4. 124
5. 306
6. 5·35
7. 4·3
8. 17·8
9. 0·82
10. 316·5

Make these numbers 10 times smaller.

11. 30
12. 70
13. 120
14. 56
15. 42
16. 5·6
17. 13·6
18. 74·5
19. 0·8
20. 1·7

Make these numbers 100 times larger.

21. 4
22. 14
23. 37
24. 87
25. 90
26. 4·26
27. 8·6
28. 14·6
29. 0·38
30. 1·9

Make these numbers 100 times smaller.

31. 100
32. 500
33. 3700
34. 9000
35. 750
36. 56
37. 78
38. 129
39. 402
40. 108

Write these as decimals.

41. $4\frac{1}{2}$
42. $1\frac{3}{4}$
43. $2\frac{1}{4}$
44. $17\frac{1}{2}$
45. $25\frac{1}{4}$
46. $5\frac{7}{10}$
47. $8\frac{3}{4}$
48. $11\frac{1}{10}$
49. $7\frac{9}{10}$
50. $3\frac{3}{10}$
51. $14\frac{1}{4}$
52. $6\frac{1}{5}$
53. $15\frac{1}{2}$
54. $2\frac{3}{5}$
55. $1\frac{4}{5}$

Number and Algebra

Which numbers do the letters point to?

1.

2.

3.

4.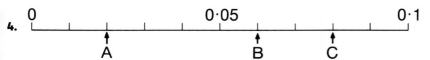

5.

Try these.

6. $\begin{array}{r} 4\cdot75 \\ +\ 3\cdot6 \\ \hline \end{array}$	**7.** $\begin{array}{r} 8\cdot0 \\ -\ 4\cdot7 \\ \hline \end{array}$	**8.** $\begin{array}{r} 6\cdot5 \\ +\ 8\cdot5 \\ \hline \end{array}$	**9.** $\begin{array}{r} 9\cdot36 \\ -\ 2\cdot81 \\ \hline \end{array}$	**10.** $\begin{array}{r} 4\cdot6 \\ -\ 1\cdot9 \\ \hline \end{array}$

11. $\begin{array}{r} 5\cdot73 \\ +\ 1\cdot92 \\ \hline \end{array}$	**12.** $\begin{array}{r} 8\cdot59 \\ -\ 2\cdot7 \\ \hline \end{array}$	**13.** $\begin{array}{r} 9\cdot04 \\ -\ 6\cdot5 \\ \hline \end{array}$	**14.** $\begin{array}{r} 3\cdot4 \\ +\ 2\cdot69 \\ \hline \end{array}$	**15.** $\begin{array}{r} 8\cdot14 \\ -\ 2\cdot75 \\ \hline \end{array}$

16. $\begin{array}{r} 6\cdot4 \\ \times\quad 7 \\ \hline \end{array}$	**17.** $\begin{array}{r} 9\cdot6 \\ \times\quad 5 \\ \hline \end{array}$	**18.** $\begin{array}{r} 4\cdot8 \\ \times\quad 9 \\ \hline \end{array}$	**19.** $\begin{array}{r} 5\cdot18 \\ \times\quad 6 \\ \hline \end{array}$	**20.** $\begin{array}{r} 3\cdot6 \\ \times\quad 8 \\ \hline \end{array}$

21. $4\overline{)16\cdot84}$ **22.** $8\overline{)28\cdot8}$ **23.** $9\overline{)77\cdot49}$ **24.** $6\overline{)34\cdot2}$ **25.** $7\overline{)65\cdot1}$

Calculator

Start with 100 on the display each
time. You are only allowed to divide.
Try to show these.

1.
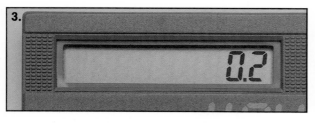

2.
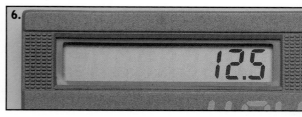

3.
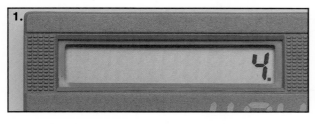

4.

5.
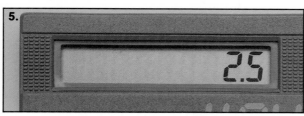

6.
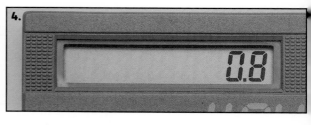

7.

8.

9.

10.

Can you do the same with a starting number of 50 ?

Calculator

Complete the sequence without using the calculator.

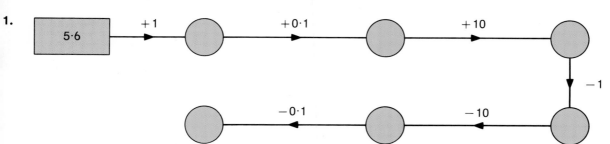

1.

Now check with the calculator.

Do these without the calculator.

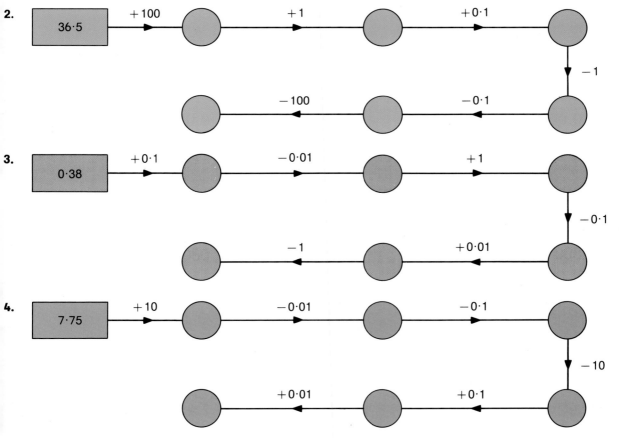

2.

3.

4.

Now check with the calculator.

Measures

Is it 8 o'clock in the morning
or evening?

So that people catch their buses,
trains and aeroplanes on time,
all timetables use the **24 hour clock**.

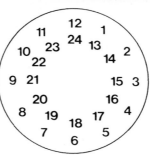

8.00 am is written 0800	11.00 am is written 1100
8.00 pm is written 2000	11.00 pm is written 2300

Write these as 24 hour clock times.

1. 10.00 am   2. 2.00 pm   3. 6.00 am   4. 9.00 pm   5. 6.00 pm

6. 11.00 pm   7. 3.00 am   8. 7.00 pm   9. 1.00 pm   10. 5.00 am

Write these 24 hour clock times using am and pm.

11. 1400   12. 0600   13. 0900   14. 2100   15. 1700

16. 2300   17. 0100   18. 1600   19. 0800   20. 1200

9.15 am is written 0915	4.35 am is written 0435
9.15 pm is written 2115	4.35 pm is written 1635

Write these as 24 hour clock times.

21. 2.40 am   22. 6.20 pm   23. 11.50 am   24. 7.45 pm   25. 3.05 am

26. 10.20 pm   27. 9.40 pm   28. 6.55 am   29. 12.15 pm   30. 11.50 pm

Write these times using am and pm.

1. 1640	2. 0720	3. 0115	4. 2135	5. 1245

6. 0350   7. 2205   8. 1720   9. 1155   10. 1015

11. 0240   12. 1515   13. 1310   14. 0750   15. 2355

16. Copy and complete this table.

half past 6 in the morning	6.30 am	0630
$\frac{1}{4}$ to 4 in the afternoon	3.45 pm	1545
10 to 5 in the afternoon		
		0740
	8.50 pm	
25 to 11 in the morning		
	6.15 pm	
15 minutes past midday		
		1915
	12.05 am	

17. A train leaves Totley at 0710 and arrives at Woolbridge at 1340. How long was the train travelling?

18. An hour and a half after starting from Totley, the train arrives at Poolgate. What time did the train arrive at Poolgate?

19. Five minutes later the train travels to Handley. It arrives at 1135. How long did it take the train to travel from Poolgate to Handley?

20. One hour fifty minutes after arriving at Handley, the train arrives at Western Bay. What time did the train arrive at Western Bay?

CHESTERFIELD ● WINGERWORTH   Complete Service   Service 34

Mondays to Saturdays

CHESTERFIELD (EM Bus Stn.)	0620	0645	0655	0715	0735	0745	0755	0835	0850	0855	0910	0935	1021	1035	1051
Langer Lane Terminus	0630	......	0705	......	0745	......	0805	0845	0900	0905	......	0945	......	1045	......
Wingerworth (Lido)	0634	0659	0709	0729	0749	0759	0809	0849	0904	0909	0925	0949	1035	1049	1106
TUPTON (Four Lane Ends)	0637	......	0712	......	0752	......	0812	0852	0907	0912	0928	0952	1038	1052	1109

CHESTERFIELD (EM Bus Stn.)	1105	1135	1205	1221	1235	1321	1335	1351	1405	1435	1505	1521	1535	1621	1635
Langer Lane Terminus	1115	1145	1215	......	1245	......	1345	......	1415	1445	1515	......	1545	......	1645
Wingerworth (Lido)	1119	1149	1219	1235	1249	1335	1349	1406	1419	1449	1519	1535	1549	1635	1649
TUPTON (Four Lane Ends)	......	1152	......	1238	1252	1338	1352	1409	......	1452	......	1538	1552	1638	1652

CHESTERFIELD (EM Bus Stn.)	1652	1701	1715	1735	1745	1805	1835	1908	1935	2008	2108	2205	2235	2305
Langer Lane Terminus	1702	......	......	1745	......	1815	1845	......	1945	......	......	2215	......	2315
Wingerworth (Lido)	1706	1716	1730	1749	1759	1819	1849	1922	1949	2022	2122	2219	2249	2319
TUPTON (Four Lane Ends)	1709	1719	1733	1752	......	......	1852	......	1952	......	......	2222	......	2322

1. How long does it take for a bus to travel from Chesterfield to Tupton?

2. How long does it take for a bus to travel from Chesterfield to Wingerworth?

3. How many minutes does it take a bus to travel from Wingerworth to Tupton?

4. If I catch a bus leaving Langer Lane Terminus at 1645, what time will I arrive at Tupton?

5. Richard is having a birthday party at 4.00 pm. He lives at Wingerworth. Which bus must I catch from Chesterfield to get there in time?

6. What is the time of the last bus from Chesterfield to Tupton?

7. My mother went shopping in Chesterfield.
She arrived at Chesterfield at 2.00 pm and spent $2\frac{1}{2}$ hrs shopping.
Which bus would she catch home to Wingerworth?

This map shows the bus routes connecting several towns. All buses travelling between the towns travel at an average speed of 30 mph.

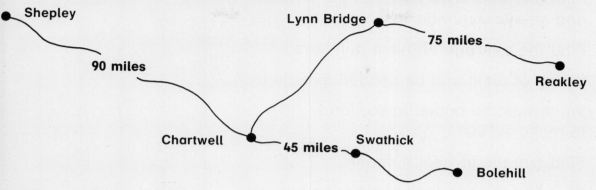

Shepley

90 miles

Lynn Bridge

75 miles

Reakley

Chartwell

45 miles

Swathick

Bolehill

1. The bus from Chartwell to Shepley leaves Chartwell at 0940. What time does it arrive at Shepley?

2. It takes $2\frac{1}{2}$ hrs from Chartwell to Lynn Bridge. How far is it from Chartwell to Lynn Bridge?

3. A non-stop bus to Chartwell leaves Reakley at 0950. What time does it arrive at Chartwell?

4. If it takes $1\frac{1}{2}$ hrs to travel between Swathick and Bolehill, how far is it from Chartwell to Bolehill?

5. How long would it take an express bus (no stops) from Bolehill to Chartwell?

6. An express bus to Chartwell leaves Bolehill at 1830. What time does it arrive at Chartwell?

Number and Algebra

1. Find the total of these numbers.

2. Find the difference between the largest and smallest numbers.

3. Find the average of these numbers.

4. Which of them can be divided exactly by 4.

5. What must be added to the total to make 10000?

6. Find $\frac{3}{4}$ of the largest number.

7. Find $\frac{2}{3}$ of the smallest number.

```
  462
 1583
 6004
   87.
 1414
```

8. Find the total of these amounts.

9. Which amount is 48p less than £10?

10. Which amount is double another amount?

11. Which two amounts, when added, come to less than £5?

12. Subtract the next to smallest amount from the largest amount.

13. Find the average of the five amounts.

```
£8.70
£6.08
£9.52
£4.35
£0.60
```

This dial shows the miles travelled by a car.

14. Its last journey was 189 miles. What did the dial show before that journey?

15. The average mileage travelled each week is 100 miles. How many weeks old is the car?

16. Its next journey will be 104 miles. What will the dial show then?

> Remember
> the sign > means is greater than
> the sign < means is less than
>
> $7 + 4 > 9$
> $19 - 4 < 6 \times 4$

Put the correct sign (> < =) in these:

1. $17 + 34 \ \square \ 7 \times 7$
2. $3 \times 56 \ \square \ 144 + 27$
3. $600 - 145 \ \square \ 700 - 245$
4. $500 \div 4 \ \square \ 1000 \div 8$
5. $700 \div 2 \ \square \ \frac{1}{2}$ of 698
6. $\frac{1}{8}$ of 96 $\square$ $96 \div 8$
7. $\frac{1}{3}$ of 60 $\square$ 9×3
8. $40 \times 6 \ \square \ 252 \div 6$

Use the examples to help you do these:

```
  345
+ 197
─────
  542
```

9. $542 - 197$
10. $197 + 345$
11. $542 - 345$

```
  502
- 247
─────
  255
```

12. $247 + 255$
13. $502 - 255$
14. $255 + 247$

15. Find the number which is 9 times greater than 896.

16. Which number is $\frac{2}{3}$ of 1683?

17. Find the number which is $\frac{3}{4}$ of 6464.

18. Add together $\frac{1}{3}$ of £17·10 and $\frac{3}{8}$ of £19·60.

19. Which sum of money is 6 times £4·85?

20. How many times will 7 divide into 3843?

21. Find the average of 2121, 3608, 400, 3931.

22. What is the average of £7·35, £8·42, £0·16, £3·84 and £2·08?

23. The product of two numbers is 196.
    One of the numbers is 7. Find the other number.

Mr. Jones hires out cars.
He has five cars for people to choose from.
This table shows how many miles each car will travel on 5 litres of petrol.

Car 1	Car 2	Car 3	Car 4	Car 5
28 miles	29 miles	34 miles	38 miles	44 miles

Each car has 30 litres of petrol in it.

1. Make a table to show how far each car would travel on the petrol already in it.

2. Mr. Smith hired Car 2.
    His journey was 116 miles each way.
    How much more petrol would he need?

3. Mrs. James was travelling 300 miles altogether.
    She could only afford 10 litres of petrol.
    Which cars could she choose?

4. Mr. Martin chose Car 1.
    Miss Richards chose Car 4.
    They put another 30 litres in each car.
    How much further could Miss Richards travel than Mr. Martin?

5. Make another table to show how far each car would travel on 50 litres of petrol.

Calculator

This table shows how much foreign money £1 will buy.

Australia ...2·28 dollars	Greece ....225 drachmas	Norway ....10·80 **kroner**
Austria ......20·60 schillings	Holland ....3·31 guilders	Portugal ....229 escudos
Belgium ....61·40 francs	Iceland ....63·00 kronur	South Africa .....3·50 rand
Canada .....2·1650 dollars	Ireland ....1·11 punts	Spain ....190·25 pesetas
Cyprus ......0·77 pounds	Israel ....2·50 shekels	Sweden ....10·42 kronor
Denmark ...11·33 kroner	Italy ....2120 lire	Switzerland ......2·4350 francs
Finland .....7·17 markkaa	Japan ....237 yen	Turkey ....1540 lire
France ......9·83 francs	Malta ....0·5620 pounds	United States ...1·65 dollars
Germany ..2·94 marks	New Zealand ....2·51 dollars	Yugoslavia ....1490 dinars

1. How many German marks will £50 buy?

2. How much Dutch money will £100 buy?

3. Approximately how much would 1000 French francs cost?

4. Approximately how much would 20 000 Italian lire cost?

5. You are going on holiday to Greece.
   Make a simple ready reckoner to help you.

Digit cards 0–9

Each of the digit cards has a home.
Find it.

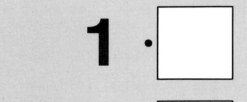

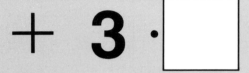

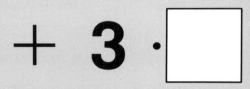

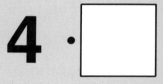

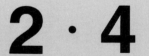

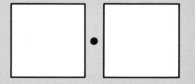

Do the same with these.

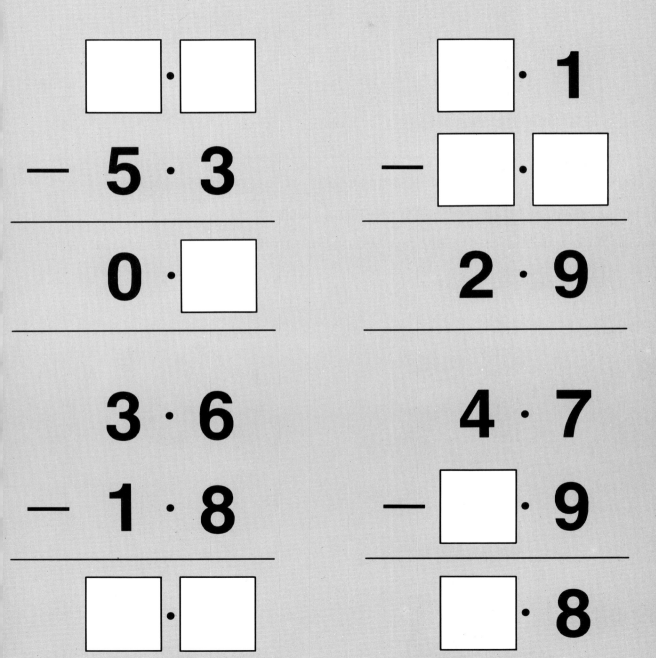

Shape and space

Each of these shapes has an area of 6 triangles.

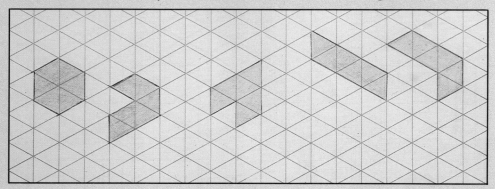

1. Can you find any more shapes with an area of 6 triangles?

2. Draw the shape with the smallest perimeter.

3. Choose one of the shapes which you think will not tessellate.
   Draw it.
   Cut it out and test it.

Squares

Here are some 6-square shapes.

1. Draw the shape with the smallest perimeter.

2. Draw the shape with most sides.

3. How many other shapes can you make from 6 squares?

4. Choose one of the shapes which you think will not tessellate.
Draw it.
Cut it out and test it.

Measures

Metre stick

Calculate the area of these rectangles.

1. 7 cm by 5 cm
2. 12 cm × 6 cm
3. 14 cm × 10 cm
4. 26 cm by 9 cm
5. 19 cm × 8 cm
6. 18 cm × 7 cm

7.

8.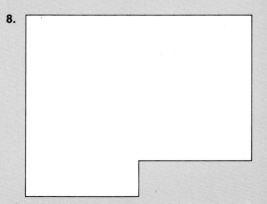

To measure a large area we use a square, 1 metre by 1 metre.
A square, 1 m by 1 m, has an area of 1 **square metre**.
We write it as 1 **m²**.

9. Use your metre stick to draw 1 m² on the classroom floor.
   Estimate the area of the classroom in m².
   Measure the length of the classroom in metres (to the nearest metre).
   Measure the width of the classroom in metres (to the nearest metre).
   Calculate the approximate area of the classroom in m².

10. In the same way, find the area of the hall or the library or the playground or any other room in the school.

11. How many cm² make 1 m²?

Calculate the area of:

1. a rectangular table 2 m by 1 m
2. a sheet of paper 10 cm by 24 cm
3. a carpet 6 m by 5 m
4. a piece of card 9 cm by 14 cm.

Find the length of:

5. a rectangle of area 80 cm² and width 5 cm
6. a carpet of area 15 m² and width 5 m
7. a garden of area 189 m² and width 9 m.

Calculate the area of each of these plots of land.
The scale for each drawing is shown.

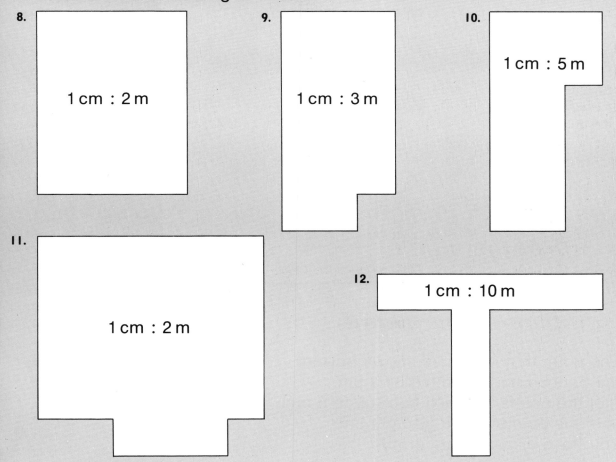

8.

1 cm : 2 m

9.

1 cm : 3 m

10.

1 cm : 5 m

11.

1 cm : 2 m

12.

1 cm : 10 m

Handling data

Mr. North has a hot air balloon. He travels long distances in it.
It travels at a steady 10 km an hour. (1 km = 1000 m)

He set off one day at noon for an 8 hour flight.
This table shows how far he travelled each hour.

Time	Noon	1 pm	2 pm	3 pm	4 pm	5 pm	6 pm	7 pm	8 pm
Distance travelled in km	0	10	20	30	40	50	60	70	80

Copy this graph into your book.

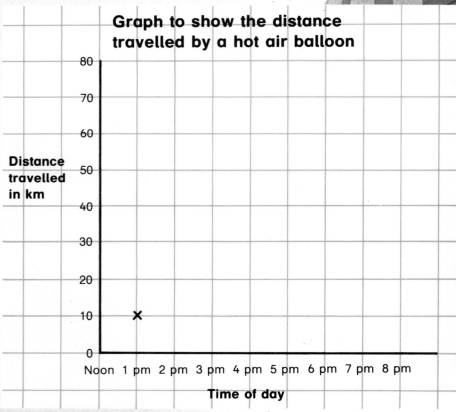

The point that is plotted shows how far
the balloon had travelled by 1 pm.
Plot the points for each hour up to 8 pm.
Join the points with a straight line.
You have drawn a **line graph**.

Mr. Leggit is a long-distance walker.
He walks 5 miles in an hour.
He set off one Saturday to walk from Derby to Sheffield.
The distance he had to walk was 40 miles.
This is the route he took. The numbers show the miles between towns.

| Derby | —8— | Belper | —2— | Ambergate | —8— | Matlock | —7— | Chatsworth | —2— | Baslow | —13— | Sheffield |

1. Complete this table to show how far he travelled each hour.

Number of hours	1	2	3	4	5	6	7	8
Distance in miles	5	10						

2. Draw a line graph of the distance travelled each hour.

Answer these questions from the graph.

3. How far had he walked in
   (a) $3\frac{1}{2}$ hours?   (b) $6\frac{1}{2}$ hours?

4. How long did it take him to walk
   (a) $12\frac{1}{2}$ miles?   (b) $37\frac{1}{2}$ miles?

Answer these questions from the plan of the route.

5. How long did it take him to walk
   (a) from Derby to Ambergate?
   (b) from Ambergate to Chatsworth?
   (c) from Chatsworth to Sheffield?

6. If he left Derby at 10 o'clock, at what time did he reach
   (a) Belper?   (b) Chatsworth?   (c) Baslow?

Tennis ball

Drop a tennis ball from a height of 1 metre.
How high does it bounce?
It will help if you do this beside a wall.
Repeat it nine more times.

Draw a stick graph to show the height of each bounce.

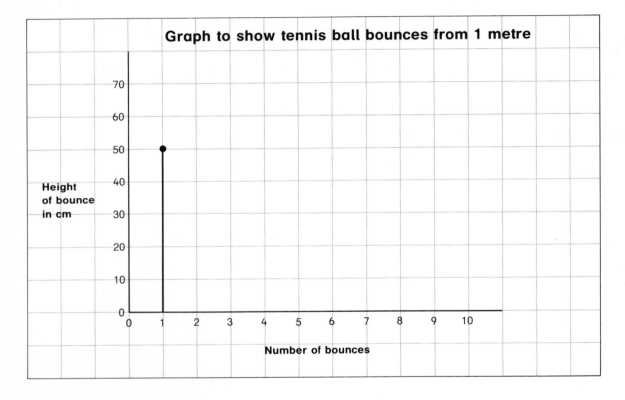

Find the average height of bounce.

To find the average:
add together the heights of the 10 bounces
divide this total by 10.

Table-tennis ball, golf ball, rubber ball, plastic ball, metre stick

Which is the best bouncer?

Drop a table-tennis ball from a height of 1 metre.
How high does it bounce?
Repeat this five more times.
Find the average height the ball bounces.

Repeat this activity for the other balls.

Draw a stick graph to show the **average** height each ball bounces.

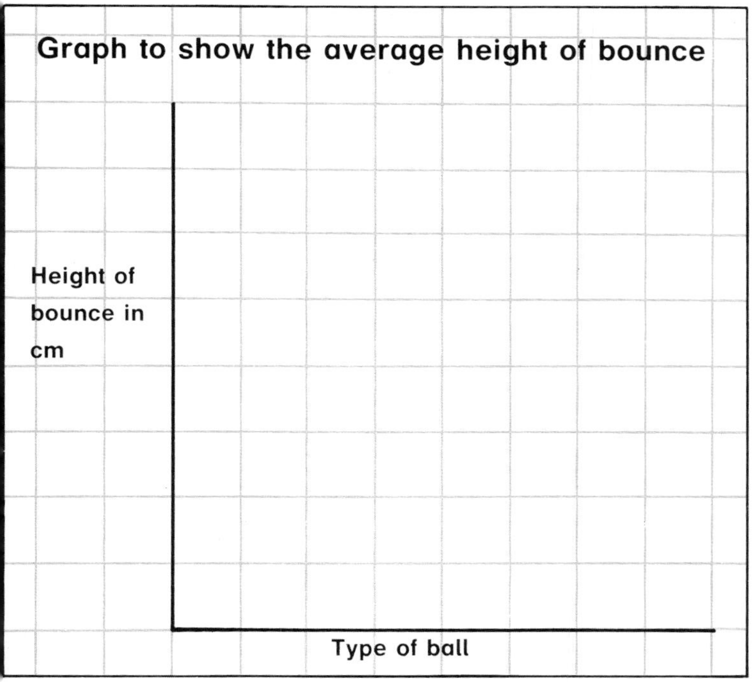

Graph to show the average height of bounce

Height of
bounce in
cm

Type of ball

Puzzles

Matchsticks, counters, squared paper

Puzzle it out

1. Take away 5 matchsticks to leave 3 squares of the same size.

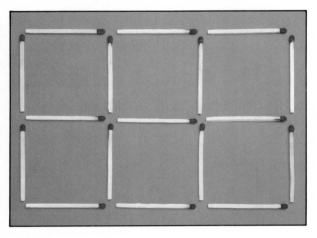

2. Copy this star without taking your pencil off the paper and without going over the same line twice.

3. Copy this into your book. Draw 3 straight lines which will separate the 7 mice from each other.

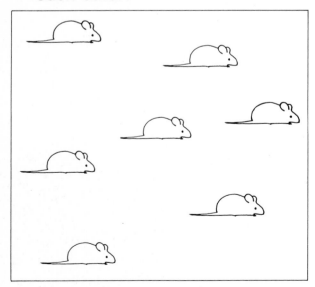

4. Rearrange the counters so that no more than 2 counters are in a straight line.

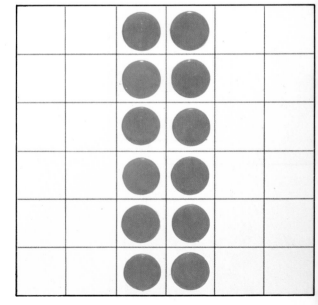

112

Mirror

Move a mirror over the page.
Try to find the hidden words.

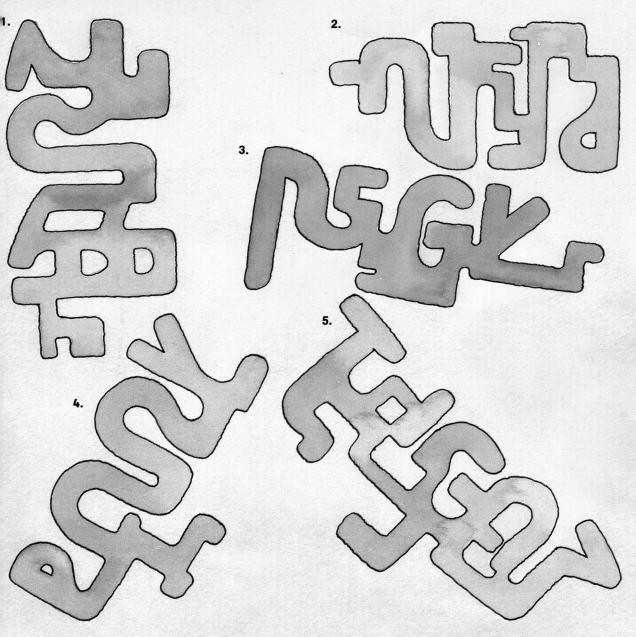

1.

2.

3.

4.

5.

Make some puzzle words of your own.

Measures

Set square, compasses

Copy these drawings.
Be as accurate as you can.

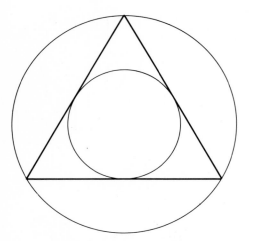
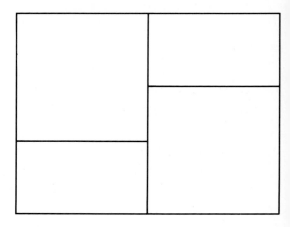

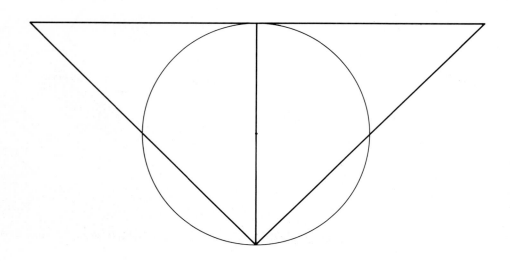

Set square, cm cubes

1. Draw a 50 mm square.
   Draw a square twice this size.
   Is the perimeter twice as big?
   Is the area twice as big?

2. Draw a 40 mm by 60 mm rectangle.
   Draw a rectangle twice the size.
   Is the perimeter twice as big?
   Is the area twice as big?

3. Make a 2 cm cube from cm cubes.
   Make a cube with each face twice as long.
   Do you need twice as many cubes?

4. Make a 2 cm × 3 cm × 4 cm cuboid from cm cubes.
   Make a cuboid with each face twice as big.
   Do you need twice as many cubes?

Micrometer, feeler gauges

Use a micrometer.
Measure the thickness
of some objects.

Use some feeler gauges.
Measure the gaps in
some objects.

Depth gauge, graduated caliper

Use a depth gauge.
Measure the depths of
some containers.

Use a graduated caliper.
Measure the thickness
or the diameter of some
objects.

3 small boxes, centimetre cubes

Choose one of the boxes.
Put a layer of cubes in the bottom of the box.
Record how many cubes are in one layer.

Find how many layers are needed to fill the box.
Record the number of layers in the box.

What is the total number of cubes in the box?

The number of cm cubes that a box holds is called its **volume.**

Find the volumes of the other two boxes.
Write your answers like this:

Number of cubes in a layer ☐

Number of layers ☐

Volume ☐ cm cubes

The volume of 1 **cm cube** is written as 1 **cm³.**

Calculate the volumes of these boxes.
Write your answers like this:

Number of cubes in a layer ☐

Number of layers ☐

Volume ☐ cm³

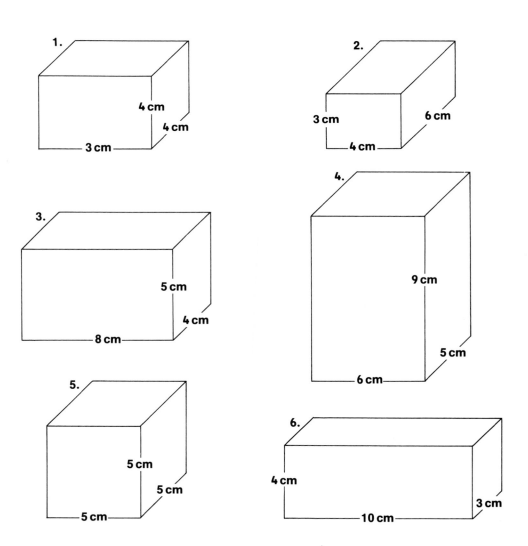

1. 4 cm 4 cm 3 cm

2. 3 cm 6 cm 4 cm

3. 5 cm 4 cm 8 cm

4. 9 cm 5 cm 6 cm

5. 5 cm 5 cm 5 cm

6. 4 cm 10 cm 3 cm

Number of cubes in a layer   20
Number of layers   6
Volume   120 cm³

Area of base   20 cm²
Height   6 cm
Volume   120 cm³

The volume of a cuboid can be found by multiplying the area of its base by its height.

Calculate the volumes of these boxes.
Write your answers like this:

Area of base = ☐ cm²

Height = ☐ cm

Volume = ☐ cm³

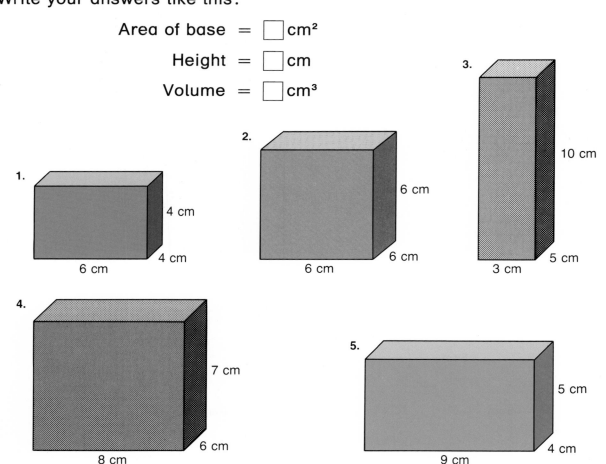

1. 6 cm, 4 cm, 4 cm

2. 6 cm, 6 cm, 6 cm

3. 3 cm, 10 cm, 5 cm

4. 8 cm, 7 cm, 6 cm

5. 9 cm, 5 cm, 4 cm

1. The volume is 60 cm³.
   What is the area of the base?
   What is the width?

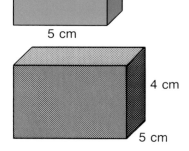

3 cm

5 cm

2. The volume is 120 cm³.
   What is the area of the base?
   What is the length?

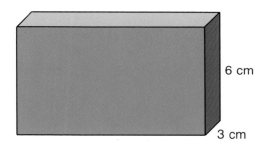

4 cm

5 cm

3. The volume is 180 cm³.
   What is the area of the base?
   What is the length?

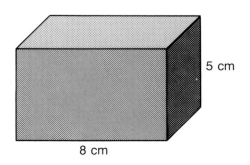

6 cm

3 cm

4. The volume is 360 cm³.
   What is the width?

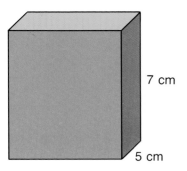

5 cm

8 cm

5. The volume is 210 cm³.
   What is the length?

7 cm

5 cm

Number and Algebra

Peg board, pegs

Make rectangles or squares with pegs.

rectangle

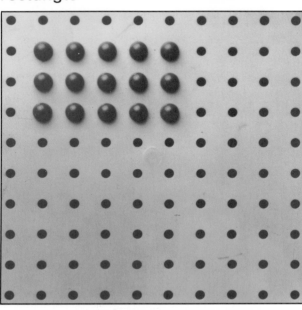

square

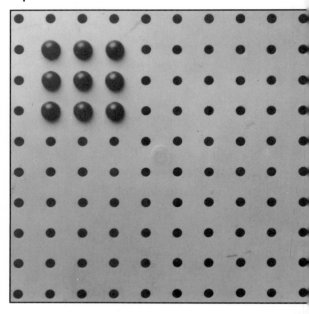

1. Which numbers make rectangles? 2. Which numbers make squares?

single line

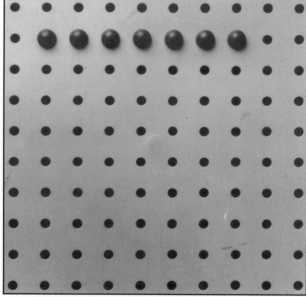

Some numbers will not make rectangles or squares.
They will only make single lines.

3. Which numbers only make single lines?

122

100 square

1	2	3	4	5	6	7	8	9	10
11	12	13	14	15	16	17	18	19	20
21	22	23	24	25	26	27	28	29	30
31	32	33	34	35	36	37	38	39	40
41	42	43	44	45	46	47	48	49	50
51	52	53	54	55	56	57	58	59	60
61	62	63	64	65	66	67	68	69	70
71	72	73	74	75	76	77	78	79	80
81	82	83	84	85	86	87	88	89	90
91	92	93	94	95	96	97	98	99	100

Cross out 1.
Cross out all the numbers divisible by 2 but not 2.
Cross out all the numbers divisible by 3 but not 3.
Cross out all the numbers divisible by 5 but not 5.
Cross out all the numbers divisible by 7 but not 7.

Make a list of all the numbers not crossed out.
These numbers are only divisible by themselves and 1.
They are called **prime numbers**.

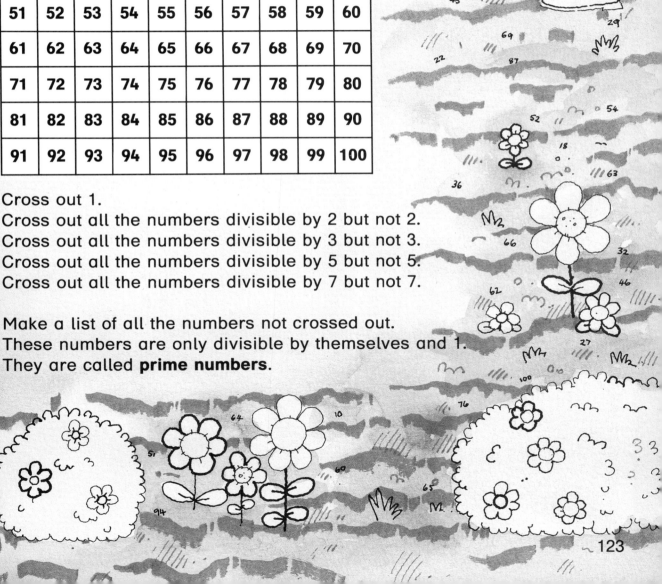

Assessment

1. $4379 + 476 + 58$

2. $1\frac{1}{2}l - 750\,ml$

3. Measure these five lines in mm.

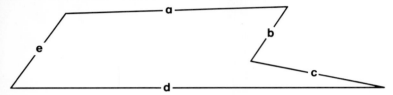

4. Find the average of 460 g, 730 g, 980 g, 370 g and 470 g.

5. $1\frac{3}{4} + \frac{1}{2}$

6. $2\frac{1}{2} - \frac{3}{4}$

7. Find $\frac{1}{8}$ of £2·64.

8. Calculate the volume of this cuboid.

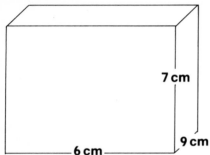

9. Calculate the area of this shape in m².

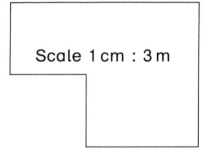

Scale 1 cm : 3 m

10. Make each of these numbers 10 times bigger: 4·3, 64·6, 108·3.

11. $13·41 + 17·8 + 3·92$

12. $15·06 - 7·3$

13. $5·4 \times 6$

16. $6·8 \div 4$

15. Write each of these times in the 24 hour clock way.
4.20 am, 6.55 pm, 3.05 pm.

16. Measure this angle.

17. $56 - (17 + 14)$

18. $(7 \times 8) - (3 \times 7)$

19. Which numbers do the letters point to?

20. Change $\frac{17}{4}$ into a mixed number.

21. What is the perimeter of a 7 cm square?

22. Make each of these 10 times smaller:
4·6, 13·5, 7, 1·25.

Put in the missing sign, $>$, $<$ or $=$.

23. $3\frac{1}{2}$ ☐ $3·45$

24. $1\frac{3}{4}$ m ☐ 190 cm

25. $1\frac{1}{4}$ kg ☐ 1250 g

26. $4·1$ ☐ $4·37$

27. Is this triangle isosceles, equilateral or scalene?

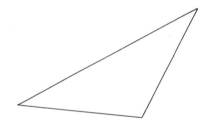

28. The volume is 250 cm³.
What is the width?

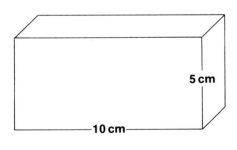

29. The area is 108 m².
What is the length?

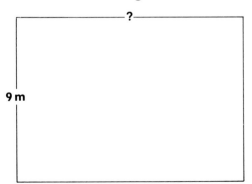

30. How many minutes is it from 2105 hrs to 2132 hrs?

Glossary

acute angle	an angle measuring less than 90°
average	the average of 3, 7 and 8 is 6. (3 + 7 + 8) ÷ 3 = 6.
circumference	the perimeter of a circle
consecutive numbers	'next door' numbers (e.g. 22, 23 and 24)
co-ordinates	a pair of numbers that plot position
degree	angles are measured in degrees (e.g. 90°)
diagonal	a line across a shape from one vertex to another
diameter	a straight line through the centre of a circle
digit card	a card showing a single number (0 to 9)
equilateral triangle	a triangle with three equal sides and three equal angles
equivalent fractions	fractions that are worth the same (e.g. $\frac{1}{2} = \frac{2}{4} = \frac{4}{8}$)
isosceles triangle	a triangle with two equal sides and two equal angles
kilometre	a measure of length (1 km = 1000 m)
line of symmetry	a line which divides a shape into matching parts
millimetre	a measure of length (10 mm = 1 cm)
mixed number	a number made up of whole ones and a fraction (e.g. $1\frac{3}{4}$)
obtuse angle	an angle less than 180° and more than 90°
perimeter	the distance round a shape or object
plan	a diagram showing the position of items or places

prime number	a number which is only exactly divisible by itself and one
product	when two numbers are multiplied together the answer is called the product
protractor	used for measuring angles
radius	the distance from the centre of a circle to the circumference
right angle	an angle of 90°
Roman numeral	a numeral used in Roman times
scale	is used to change the distances on a plan to the real distances
scalene triangle	a triangle with no equal sides
second	a measure of time (60 secs = 1 min)
semi-circle	half a circle
square metre	a square 1 m by 1 m has an area of 1 square metre
square number	a square number is made by multiplying any number by itself (e.g. $1 = 1 \times 1$, $4 = 2 \times 2$, $9 = 3 \times 3$)
tessellate	to fit shapes together without gaps
triangular number	one of the numbers in the sequence 1, 3, 6, 10, 15, 21, 28, 36, etc.

Multiplication square

1	2	3	4	5	6	7	8	9	10
2	4	6	8	10	12	14	16	18	20
3	6	9	12	15	18	21	24	27	30
4	8	12	16	20	24	28	32	36	40
5	10	15	20	25	30	35	40	45	50
6	12	18	24	30	36	42	48	54	60
7	14	21	28	35	42	49	56	63	70
8	16	24	32	40	48	56	64	72	80
9	18	27	36	45	54	63	72	81	90
10	20	30	40	50	60	70	80	90	100